HarperCollins*Publishers*

First published by HarperCollins Publishers 1991

© Bartholomew 1991

Bartholomew is a Division of

HarperCollins Publishers

ISBN 0 00 458957 2

Printed and bound by HarperCollins Publishers Glasgow
Reprint 10 9 8 7 6 5 4 3 2 1

CONTENTS

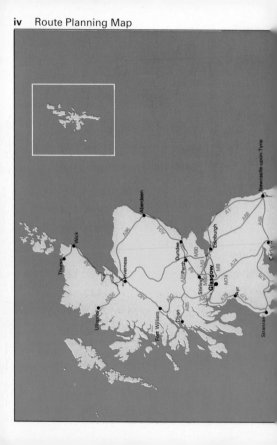

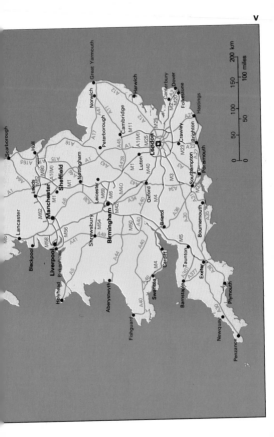

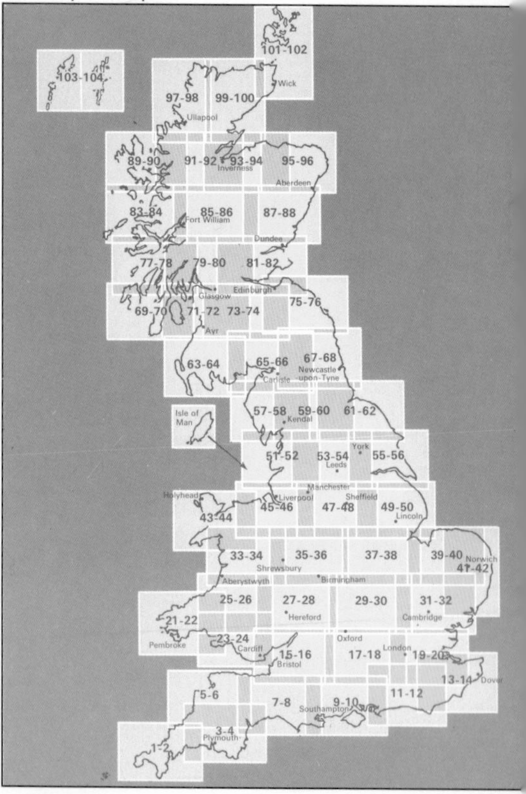
101-102
103-104
Wick
97-98
99-100
Ullapool
89-90
91-92
93-94
95-96
Inverness
Aberdeen
83-84
85-86
87-88
Fort William
Dundee
77-78
79-80
81-82
Edinburgh
Glasgow
69-70
71-72
73-74
75-76
Ayr
63-64
65-66
67-68
Newcastle
-upon-Tyne
Carlisle
Isle of
Man
57-58
59-60
61-62
Kendal
York
51-52
53-54
55-56
Leeds
Manchester
Holyhead
Liverpool
Sheffield
43-44
45-46
47-48
49-50
Lincoln
33-34
35-36
37-38
39-40
Norwich
41-42
Shrewsbury
Aberystwyth
Birmingham
25-26
27-28
29-30
31-32
Hereford
Cambridge
21-22
Pembroke
23-24
Cardiff
Oxford
London
15-16
Bristol
17-18
19-20
13-14
Dover
5-6
7-8
Southampton
9-10
11-12
3-4
Plymouth
1-2

Scale 1:760 320	12 miles to 1 inch
Junction Service Restricted Access ③─M56─⑤─ Junction under construction	motorway
	dual carriageway
─A11─ ─ ─	primary route
A529 ─ ─ ─	other 'A' roads (except P103-104)
B1010 ═ ═ ═	'B' road (P1-102), 'A' road (P103-104)
───────	'B' road (P103-104)
═ ═ ═ ═	unclassified road
───────	narrow road with passing places
6 ─●─ 31	distance in miles
～～	gradient : viewpoint
─ ─ ─➜─ ─	car ferry
▓▓▓▓▓	national boundary

⊕	airport (P1-102)	✖	motor racing circuit
✈	airport (P103-104)	♀	race course
	scenic area	⚑	golf course
	built up area	▲	youth hostel
✳	place of popular interest	╱	chairlift
～	sandy beach	3187	spot height (feet)
⚓	sailing centre		

1

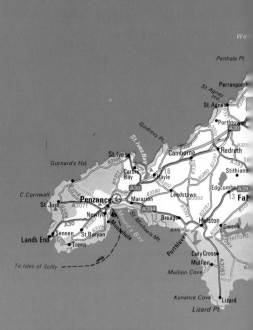

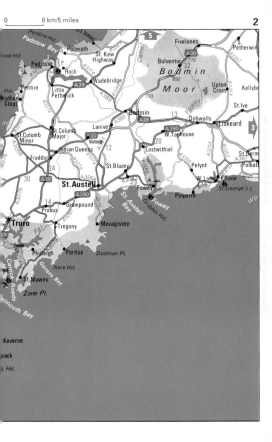

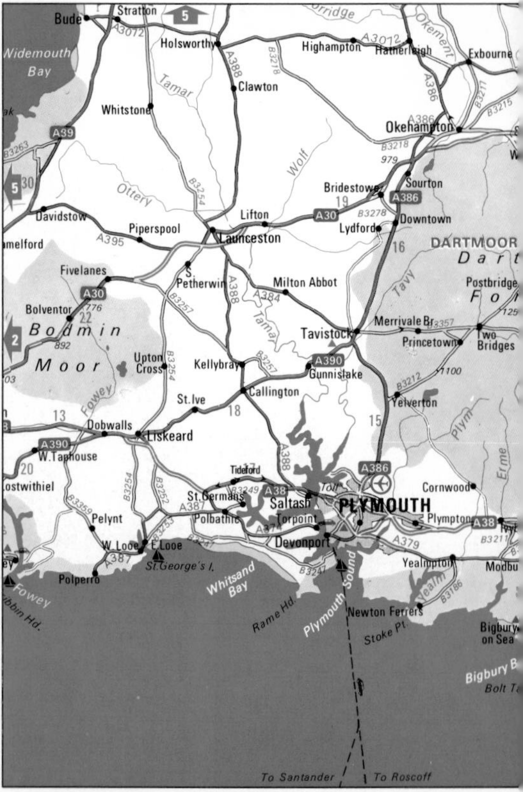

3

Bude
Stratton
5
Holsworthy
Highampton
Hatherleigh
Exbourne
Widemouth
Bay
Whitstone
Clawton
Okehampton
Davidstow
Piperspool
Lifton
A30
Downtown
-melford
Fivelanes
Bolventor
Bodmin
Moor
Upton
Cross
Kellybray
Callington
Gunnislake
Tavistock
Merrivale Br
Princetown
Two
Bridges
Postbridge
Dart
DARTMOOR
Sourton
Bridestowe
Lydford
Milton Abbot
Petherwin
Launceston
St.Ive
Dobwalls
Liskeard
W.Taphouse
-ostwithiel
Pelynt
Polbathic
St.Germans
Tideford
Saltash
Torpoint
Devonport
PLYMOUTH
Plympton
Cornwood
Yealmpton
Modbury
Yelverton
W.Looe
E.Looe
St.George's I.
Polperro
Whitsand
Bay
Rame Hd.
Plymouth Sound
Newton Ferrers
Stoke Pt.
Bigbury
on Sea
Bigbury B
Bolt Ta
Fowey
Gribbin Hd.
To Santander
To Roscoff

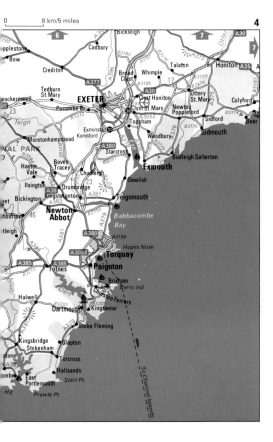

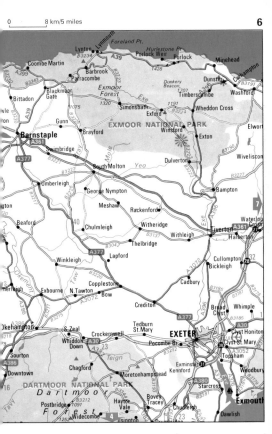

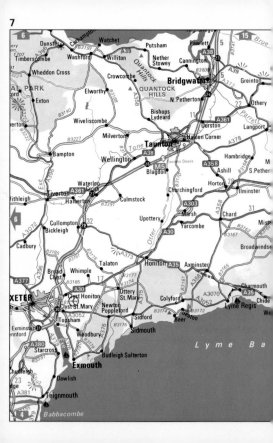

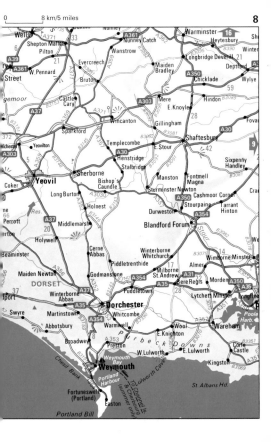

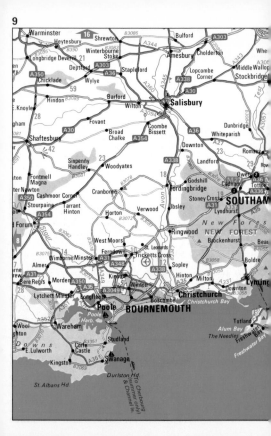

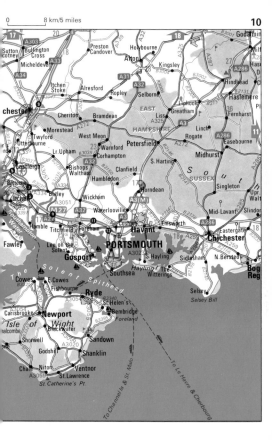

Hartley Wintney
Fleet
Odiham
Aldershot
Farnborough
Guildford
Old Woking
Mayford
Ripley
E. Clandon
E. Horsley
Merrow
Shere
Albury
Shalford
Bramley
Godalming
Dorking
Leatherhead
Mickleham
Ashtead
Reigate
Farnham
Hog's Back
SURREY
HILLS
Leith Hill
Milford
Hascombe
Dunsfold
Chiddingfold
Cranleigh
Ewhurst
Ockley
Capel
Gatwick
Charlwood
Kingsfold
Crawley
Warnham
Horsham
Alford
Crossways
Bucks Green
Plaistow
Wisborough Green
Billingshurst
Coolham
Cowfold
Kingsley
Hindhead
Haslemere
Selborne
Liphook
Greatham
Liss
Fernhurst
Linch
Rogate
Easebourne
EAST
HAMPSHIRE
Petersfield
Midhurst
Petworth
Fittleworth
Pulborough
S. Harting
South Downs
SUSSEX
Singleton
Upr. Waltham
DOWNS
Storrington
Washington
Steyning
Findon
Henfield
Muddles
Horndean
Mid-Lavant
Slindon
Arundel
Emsworth
Havant
Chichester
Eastergate
Broadwater
Sompting
Worthing
Shoreham by Sea
Littlehampton
PORTSMOUTH
S. Hayling
Hayling I.
Sidlesham
N. Bersted
Felpham
Bognor Regis
The Witterings
Selsey
Selsey Bill
A3
A31
A32
A24
A25
A27
A29
A272
A283
A285
A286
A287
A281
A323
A325
A259
A280
A264
A246
A279
B2131
B2146
B2141
B2138
B2139
B2132
B2140
B2145
B2166
B3001
B3002
B3004
B3006
B2128
B2127
B2130
B2133
B2224
B2135

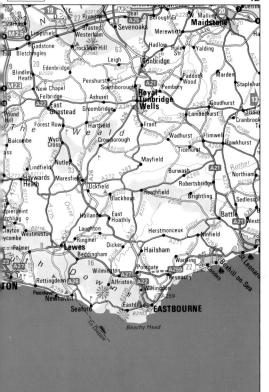

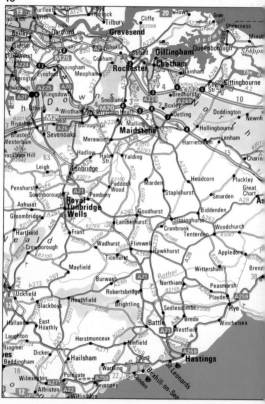

0   8 km/5 miles

To Vlissingen

Westgate on Sea   **Margate**
Kingsgate
North Foreland
Broadstairs
Ramsgate

sdown
Herne Bay   Reculver
Whitstable
Herne
Upstreet
Birchington
I. of Thanet
Sarre
Minster
am
Blean
Sturry
Wingham
Stour
Pegwell Bay
Richborough

Canterbury
Littlebourne
Ash
Sandwich

nam
Aylesham
Eastry
Deal
Walmer

DOWNS
Denton
Selstad
Elham
Lyminge
Alkham
Temple Ewell
St Margarets at Cliffe
South Foreland
To Zeebrugge
To Oostende

Dunkerque

Sellindge
Newingreen
Lympne
Hythe
Sandgate
Folkestone
Dover
To Calais

itary Canal
used)
Dymchurch
ychurch

St Mary's Bay
Littlestone-on-Sea
Greatstone-on-Sea

Dungeness

STRAIT OF DOVER

To Boulogne

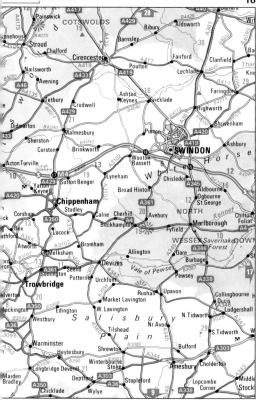

8 km/5 miles

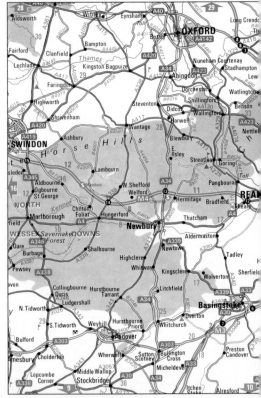

8 km/5 miles

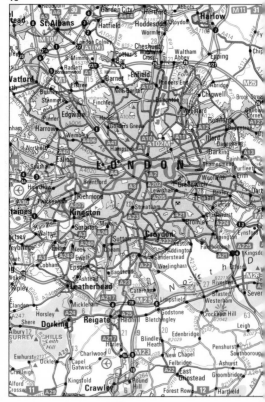

0 8 km/5 miles

roomfield · Hatfield · D'Arcy · Tollesbury · W.Mersea
Peverel · Sales Pt.
elmsford · Maldon · Blackwat
rittle · Danbury · Bradwell on Sea
Baddow · A414 · Steeple
Stock · Cold Norton · Southminster
Rettendon · Althorne · Burnham
Billericay · Wickford · on Crouch
Rochford · Foulness Pt.
ood · Hayleigh · Crouch
east · Basildon · Pitsea · Hadleigh · Gt. Wakering
Horndon · Vange · on Sea · SOUTHEND
Corryton · Canvey · ON-SEA · Shoeburyness
Stanford · Allhallows · Shoebury Ness
le Hope · Thames · Grain
rock · Tilbury · Cliffe · To Vlissingen
Gravesend · Hoo · Medway · Sheerness
Shorne · Strood · Gillingham · Queenborough · Minster · Eastchurch
obham · Rochester · Chatham · Sheppey · Leysdown · Herne Bay
Rainham · The Swale · Herne
Snodland · Bredhurst · Sittingbourne · Faversham · Whitstable
Wrotham Heath · Boxley · A2 · Blean · Sturry
M20 · Detling · Doddington · Newnham · Canterbury
Malling · Maidstone · Hollingbourne · Chilham
Lenham · KENT
Hale · Yalding · Harrietsham · Charing · DOWNS
Str · Elhan
Marden · Headcorn · Pluckley · Great · Ashford · Ly
Paddock · Staplehurst · Smarden · Chart
Wood · Biddenden · Sellindge
mbury · Goudhurst · Sissinghurst · Newingreen
ge · Lamberhurst · Cranbrook · Tenterden · Woodchurch · Ham · Lympne
Street

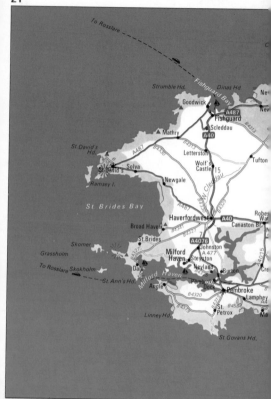

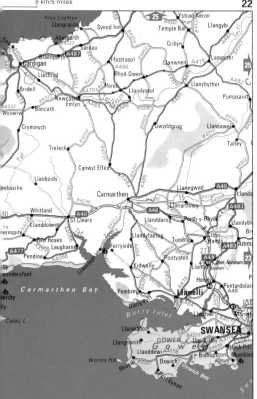

8 km/5 miles

Ynys Lochtyn
Llangranog
Aberporth
Sarnau
Blaenporth
Cardigan
Llechryd
Bridell
Boncath
Wyswyn
Crymmych

Synod Inn
Temple Bar
Cribyn
Ffostrasol
Rhyd-Owen
Horeb
Newcastle
Emlyn

Ystrad Aeron
Llangybi
Llanwnen
Lampeter
Llanybyther
Pumpsaint

Llandyssul
Llanbyther
Gwyddgrug
Llansawel
Talley

Trelech
Cynwyl Elfed

ndissilio
Llanboidy

Carmarthen

Llanegwad
Llanarthney
Porth-y-Rhyd
Whitland
St.Clears
Llanddowror
ernspite
Red Roses
Laugharne
Pendine
aunderstoot

Llansteph
Ferryside
Kidwelly

Llandyfaelog
Tumble
Cross
Hands
Pontyates

Llandybie
Bro
Amma

Pont Abraham

Pembrey
Burry Port
Llanelli
Hendy
Pontardulais
Llwchwr
Worms

Carmarthen Bay

Burry Inlet

Caldy I.
Llanmadoc
Llangennith
GOWER
Llanddewi
Rhoss
Oxwich
Port Eynon

Upr Killay
Bishopston
Oxwich Bay

SWANSEA
Black Pill
Mumbles

Worms Hd.

Swa

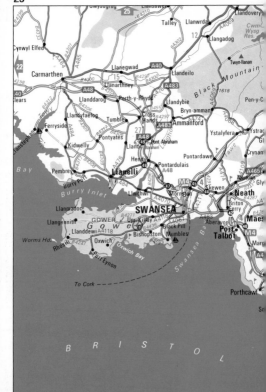

0   8 km/5 miles

St. Devere

26
A470
Talgarth
1060
A470   Llangorse   Black
Sennybridge   Llanthony   Pontrilas
astle   Usk   A479   Llangorse L.
Brecon   Llanfrynach
A4215   A470   Mountains   24
Brecon   A40   Bwlch   Tretower   Pandy   Grosmont
Brecon   Beacons   Crickhowell   Llanfihangel
BRECON   BEACONS   A4078   Crucorney
STOREY   Arms   Gilwern   A465   A4251   Llanvetherine
NATIONAL   PARK   27
A470   Taf Fechan   Brynmawr   Abergavenny   A465
(Resr.)
ont Nedd   Penderyn   Dowlais   19   Tredegar   Blaenavon   A40   Raglan
sched   Hirwaun   A465   A4060   Rhymney   Ebbw Vale   A4042
MERTHYR   11
Aberdare   TYDFIL   Abertillery   Pontypool   A449
Troed-y-rhiw   Abersychan   A472   Usk
Mountain   A470   Bargoed   Llandegfedd
ondda   Ash   Nelson   Blackwood   Res.
abergwynfi   Maerdy   A4257   Newbridge   Cwmbran   15
Rhondda   Porth   Abercarn   A449
arw   Nant-y-moel   Pontypridd   Cwmcarn   Caerleon   Per
A4064   Gilfach   A472   Cross   A4042   A48   A554
Goch   Tonyrefail   Caerphilly   Keys   27   NEWPORT   Ma
A4093   Nantgarw   Machen   28
Bryncethin   Llantrisant   A470   Taff's   A469   Castleton
 s Park   Coychurch   A4119   Whitchurch   St. Mellons
Ewenny   A48   Llandaff
Nash   Bonvilston   St. Nicholas   Wenvoe   CARDIFF   Clevedon   20
Wick   Cowbridge   A48   A4050   Penarth   Portis   6
antwit Major   A4226   Barry   A370
sh Pt.   Aberthaw   Lavernock Pt.   Worle   21
Flat Holme   Weston-   A371
Steep Holme   super-Mare   Churc
A368
Boweli
HANNEL   15

8 km/5 miles

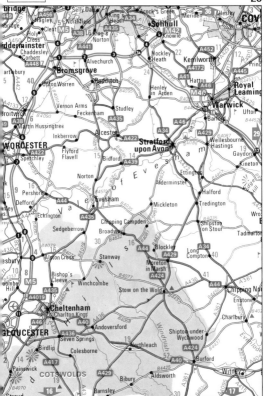

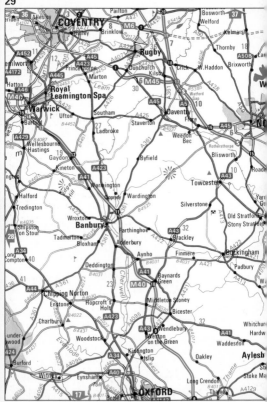

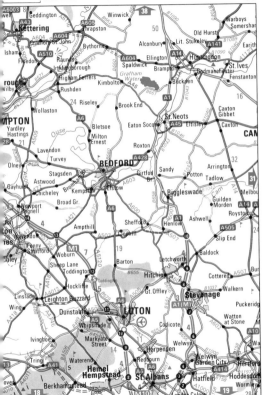

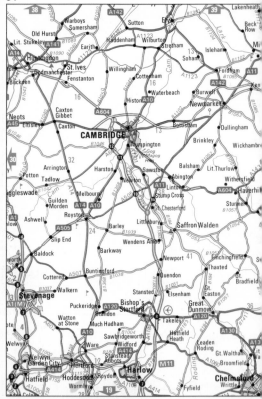

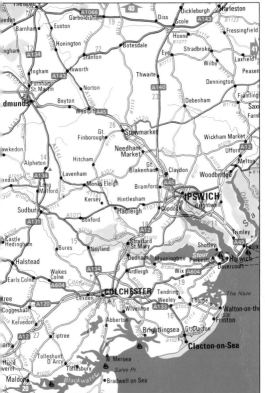

0   8 km/5 miles

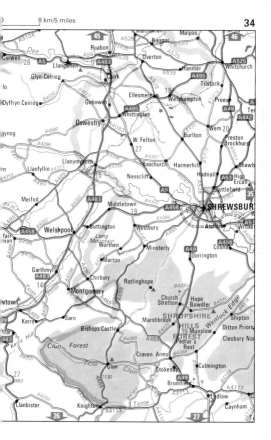

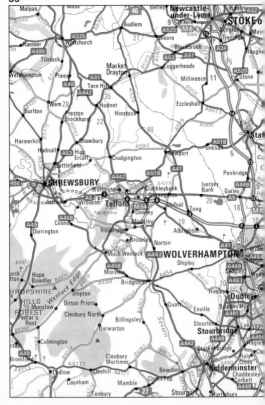

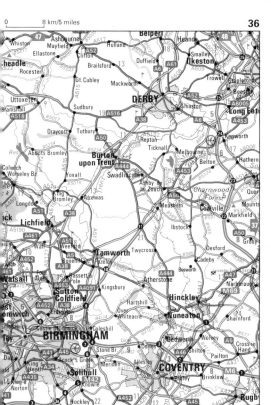

0   8 km/5 miles

A6097
Lowdham
48
Long Bennington
Bulwell
E. Bridgford
Smalley
Ilkeston
A60
NOTTINGHAM
Barkston
A609
14
Trowell
Stapleford
Whatton
Bottesford
Gt. Gonerby
Radcliffe on Trent
Bingham
A52
24
A52
Beeston
W. Bridgford
Alvaston
A6005
A46
Long Eaton
A606
Denton
5
35
A6
A453
A607
Bunny
19
Croxton Kerrial
Gt. Ponton
A1
Kegworth
15
A60
Upr. Broughton
Waltham on the Wolds
17
A6006
Rempstone
Colsterworth
Melbourne
Belton
Hathern
Wymeswold
Soar
B676
B676
21
Loughborough
A6006
Asfordby
Melton Mowbray
B675
A6
Charnwood Forest
5
Quorn
15
Mountsorrel
A46
Rearsby
A606
Gt. Dalby
10
Coalville
Langham
Markfield
11
A607
Syston
Oakham
Empingham
A50
8
Groby
LEICESTER
Tilton
Desford
Thurnby
Cadeby
A6003
A47
Preston
Morcott
Aylestone
Oadby
Billesdon
Tugby
A47
Wigston
41
Uppingham
Narborough
Great Glen
M69
Blaby
Welland
Kibworth Harcourt
15
Church Langton
Res.
Caldecott
A426
A50
Rockingham
Arnesby
A6116
24
Sharnford
11
Cottingham
Corby
Foxton
13
Wolvey
A5
M1
Lubenham
Market Harborough
Cross in Hand
Lutterworth
A427
Desborough
Shilton
Pailton
Husbands Bosworth
11
A6003
8
Geddington
A421
A426
Rothwell
A6
A43
M6
Welford
Brinklow
Kettering
Kelmarsh
A428
Broughton
36
18
A604
7
Cranford
Thornby
A45
Rugby
A5199
A508
Lamport
Isham
Finedon
A4071
Dunchurch
Crick
W. Haddon
Brixworth
Pitsford Res.
29
14
Kilsby
Marton

Weybourne
Sheringham
Blakeney Cley W. Runton Cromer
key Letheringsett A149 A148 Overstrand
Binham Holt A140
Isingham B1110 Roughton Thorpe Mundesley
37 Edgefield Green Market Paston
Saxthorpe Gunton B1150 Happisburgh
ham A149
Guist Aylsham Bure N. Walsham Palling
N. Cawston B1145 Marsham Stalham Waxha
Elmham Reepham A140 Coltishall B1151 Catfield Hor
Bawdeswell Attlebridge Horstead Hoveton The Martham
E. Wensum Horsham Wroxham Broads Bure
Dereham Hockering Drayton B1151 Ranworth Walsham A106 42
Honingham Easton A47 Yare Thorpe Biofield Acle
NORWICH Trowse Newton Yare Gor
Kimberley Hethersett A11 A146 Reedham A1
Swardeston B1108 Loddon
Hingham Wymondham Swainsthorpe Haddiscoe
Caston Ashwellthorpe A140 B1135 Wave
29 Attleborough Long Hempnall Beccles
Stratton B1332 Bungay Mettingham Nth. Co
New 20 A1
ling Buckenham Pulham Homersfield Brampton A12
E. Harling B1134 19 Wan
Kenninghall A143 Harleston Halesworth Reydon
A1066 Diss A12
oldisham 19 Dickleburgh Fressingfield Walpole Blythbrgh A106
n 22 Scole B1123 B136
Stanton Botesdale Hoxne Stradbroke Bramfield
orth 32 Eye Laxfield 41 43
Wilby Peasenhall

Bures
Stratford St Mary
Thet
E. Harling
Euston
Garboldisham
Riddlesworth
Kenninghall
Ixworth
Ixworth
Honington
Stanton
Barningham
Lavenham
Hitcham
Bildeston
Beyton
Norton
Botesdale
Thwaite
Diss
Scole
Redgrave
Harleston
Pulham
Gt. Finborough
Needham Market
Stowmarket
Thwaite
Eye
Hoxne
Stradbroke
Wilby
Brockford
Brundish
Fressingfield
Homersfield
Brampton
Hintlesham
Hadleigh
Bramford
Blakenham
Claydon
Debenham
Dennington
Laxfield
Peasenhall
Walpole
Halesworth
Rumburgh
Wrentham
IPSWICH
Woodbridge
Wickham Market
Ufford
Framlingham
Saxmundham
Cransford
Bramfield
Birthburgh
Wangford
Kessingland
Shotley
Nacton
Felixstowe
Sandlings
Debenham
Melton
Farnham
Aldringham
Leiston
Westleton
Dunwich
Walberswick
Southwold
Alderton
Bawdsey
Hollesley
Butley
Orford
Tunstall
Aldeburgh
Thorpeness
Minsmere Cliffs
Orford Ness
To Esbjerg & Göteborg
To Hamburg

Wells · Blakeney · Cley · Weybourne · Sheringham · W. Runton · Cromer · Overstrand

Market · Sheffield · Brancaster · Letheringsett · Holt · Edgefield Green · Saxthorpe · Roughton · Felbrigg · Market

Walsingham · Binham · Fakenham · Guist · Cawston · Aylsham · Thorpe Market · Southrepps · Mundesley · Paston

Shipdham · Brisley · Elmham · Bawdeswell · Reepham · Cawston · Marsham · Coltishall · W. Walsham · Stalham · Happisburgh

Watton · Caston · Hingham · Dereham · Hockering · Honingham · Attlebridge · Drayton · Horsham · Wroxham · Hoveton · The Broads · Catfield · Waxham · Sea Palling

Ashwellthorpe · Kimberley · Hethersett · **NORWICH** · Eaton · Thorpe · Trowse Newton · Brundall · Acle · Rollesby · Martham · Hemsby · Winterton

Wymondham · Swardeston · Swainsthorpe · Bixley · Blofield · Lingwood · Ranworth · Winterton

Loddon · Reedham · Filby · Ormesby St. Margaret · Caister-on-Sea

Haddiscoe · **GREAT YARMOUTH** · Gorleston · Burgh Castle · Belton · Gorton · Bradwell · To Scheveningen

Lowestoft

A11 · A140 · A47 · A146 · A148 · A149 · A1067

43

8 km/5 miles

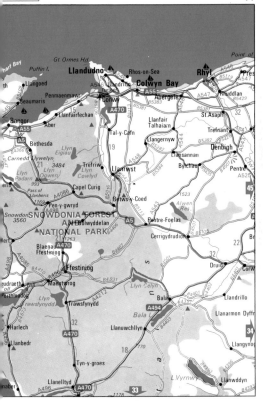

Gt Ormes Hd.
Point of
harf Bay
Puffin I.
Llandudno
Rhos-on-Sea
Rhyl
Pres
th
Llangoed
A546 Llandrillo
Colwyn Bay
B5119
A547
Penmaenmawr
Trefriw
A55
B5383
Rhuddlan
Beaumaris
Conwy
Abergele
A547
B5429
Bangor
Llanfairfechan
B5381
B5381
St.Asaph
32
A55
15
Aber
A470
Llanfair
Talhaiarn
Trefnant
A541
A5
Tal-y-Cafn
Llangernyw
A544
Bethesda
19
A548
B5382
Denbigh
A525
Carnedd Llywelyn
Llyn
Eigiau
Trefriw
Llansannan
B5382
Llyn
Padarn
3484
Llyn
Cowlyd
Llanrwst
B5384
Bytchau
Pentre
993
A525
erts
Pass of
Llanberis
Capel Curig
45
Snowdon
A4086
Betws-y-Coed
A5
Alwen
Res.
1523
3560
1168
Pen-y-gwryd
A543
SNOWDONIA FOREST
Dolwyddelan
Pentre-Foelas
AND
B4406
B4501
NATIONAL PARK
21 1263
Cerrigydrudion
22
B4104
Br
A470
Blaenau
32
Ffestiniog
Druid
Corw
Ffestiniog
B4391
n
s
B4401
udraeth
Maentwrog
Llandrillo
orthmadog
B4410
B4391
Llyn Celyn
Harlech
Trawsfynydd
B4212
A494
Llanarmon Dyffr
Bala
Llanbedr
32
Bala L.
B4403
34
Llanuwchllyn
B4401
Llangyno
18
770
Tyn-y-groes
B4405
a
B4396
B4391
A496
Llanelltyd
L.Vyrnwy
Llanwddyn
1178
B493
A470
33

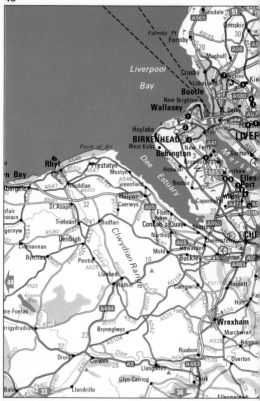

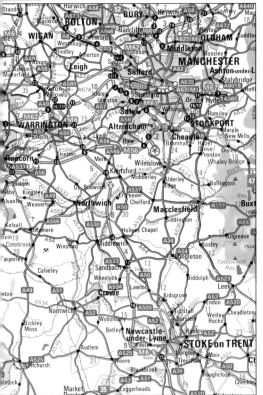

8 km/5 miles

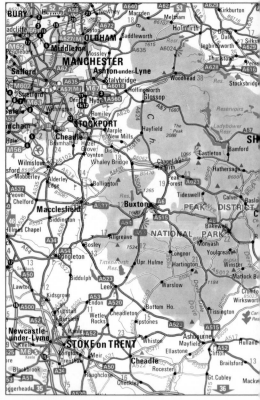

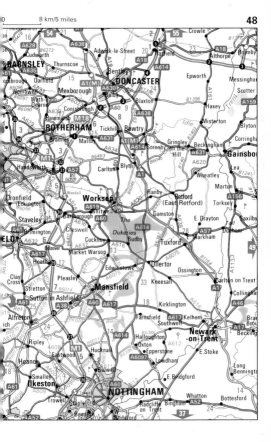

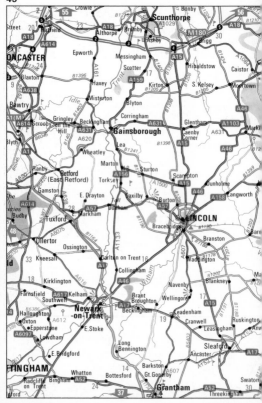

0   8 km/5 miles

50

GRIMSBY
A1098
A18 Cleethorpes
Laceby Scartho Humberston
Waltham
A16
A1031
N. Thoresby   N. Somercotes
To Rotterdam
Ludborough   Saltfleet
To Zeebrugge
Binbrook
A631
ham Louth   Grimoldby
A157
Legbourne   Mablethorpe
with LINCOLNSHIRE   Withern A157 Sutton on Sea
WOLDS   Burwell
Scamblesby   Alford A1111 Mumby
A16 A1104
A158   Ulceby Cross Chapel St. Leonards
Horncastle A1028 Willoughby
ngton Winceby A1115 Partney Burgh le Ingoldmells
42   Marsh
E. Keal   A158 Skegness
Revesby A155   Irby
l) Tumby Stickford Wainfleet
Coningsby   Gibraltar Pt.
New York Stickney
Old
Leake Wrangle
Sibsey Benington
A16 A52
A1121 Boston
sheaa A52   THE Bran
Kirton Hunstanton 39
38 A17 Sutterton   WASH Heacham 39

51

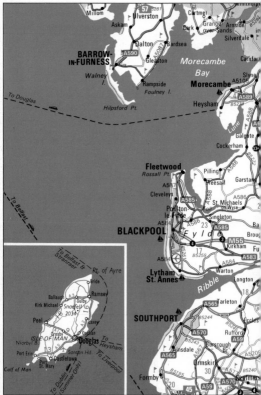

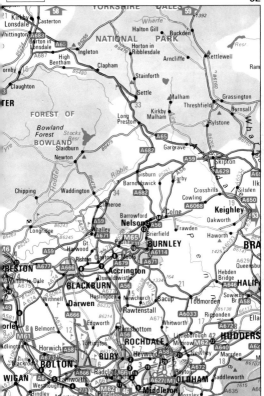

0   8 km/5 miles

YORKSHIRE DALES

58

59 1392

Kirkby Lonsdale

Casterton

Whittington

Burton in Lonsdale

Halton Gill   Buckden

A683

A65

NATIONAL   PARK

A687

Wharfe

High Bentham

Horton in Ribblesdale

Arncliffe   Kettlewell

Ingleton

Resr

ornby 16

Clapham

Stainforth

Grassington

Claughton

3

Settle

Malham

Burnsall

TER

FOREST   OF

Long Preston

33

Kirkby Malham

Threshfield

Rylstone

Bowland Forest

Stocks Resr

BOWLAND

Slaidburn

Newton

A682

Gargrave

A59

Skipton

A629

A65

yre

Hodder

Chipping

Waddington

Ribble

Gisburn

A682

Barnoldswick

Earby

Crosshills

Cowling

A6068

Silsden

A650

Keighley

A629

53

Clitheroe

34

Barrowford

Colne

Oakworth

Ilk

Longridge

Whalley

A671

Nelson

Trawden

Haworth

BRA

B6243

Gt. Harwood

A56

Brierfield

1425

B6214

A59

Rishton

Clayton le Moors

BURNLEY

A6114

A671

Hebden Bridge

Queensbu

PRESTON

A677

A666

Accrington

Oswaldtwistle

1334   764

HALIF

ton le Dale

A675

BLACKBURN

A56

Darwen

Haslingden

Newchurch

Bacup

Todmorden

A6033

Sowerby Br

Ripponden

A58

Ella

A672

Whitnell

A666

Rawtenstall

A671

Whitworth

17

orle

Belmont

Edgworth

12

Ramsbottom

ROCHDALE

Littleborough

Milnrow

Newhey

HUDDERS

A640

A62

dlington

M61

Horwich

A58

Tottington

BURY

Heywood

Boxton

Marsden

18

B6107

lackro

Westhoughton

BOLTON

A666

Farnworth

Radcliffe

M66

M62

OLDHAM

A627(M)

Saddleworth

1615

A635

WIGAN

Hindley

Atherton

M62

46

Pendlebury

Middleton

Mossley

YORKSHIRE DALES

59

60

Masha

Wharfe

1392

Halton Gill
Buckden

NATIONAL
Resr.

Horton in
Ribblesdale

Ingleton

Kettlewell

Kirkby Malzeard

PARK

Arncliffe

Clapham

Stainforth

Ramsgill

Settle

Malham

Grassington

Pateley
Bridge

Long
Preston

Kirkby
Malham

Threshfield

Burnsall

OF

33

Blubberhouses

A59

Stocks
Resr.

Gargrave

Rylstone

Wharfedale

A65

A59

Bolton Abbey

Waddington

Gisburn

A682

Skipton

A629

Ilkley

Otley

Barnoldswick

A59

Earby

Silsden

Burley

Guisele

34

Crosshills

A6068

Keighley

A650

Bingley

A658

Cowling

Whalley

Barrowford

Colne

Oakworth

Shipley

A671

Nelson

A56

Trawden

Haworth

BRADFORD

A64

Gt.
Harwood

M65

Brierfield

1425

A629

Wibsey

Pu

Rishton

Clayton-le-Moors

BURNLEY

Queensbury

A6036

Oswaldtwistle

A679

A671

A6114

Hebden
Bridge

HALIFAX

A6025

Liversedge

Heckmon

BLACKBURN

Accrington

1334

764

21

Sowerby
Br.

A58

Brighouse

A641

M

Darwen

A666

Haslingden

Newchurch

Bacup

Todmorden

A6138

Ripponden

Elland

26

A642

Floc

A666

Edgworth

Rawtenstall

A671

Whitworth

17

A6033

HUDDERSFIELD

A62

A643

A62

Ramsbottom

A56

ROCHDALE

Littleborough

Milnrow

42

Newhey

A640

Marsden

Meltham

A616

Holmfirth

Den

Da

BURY

Heywood

A58

A640

A672

Saddleworth

1615

A6024

Ingbirchworth

ON

Radcliffe

OLDHAM

A627

A62

Middleton

Mossley

47

46

M62

Pendlebu

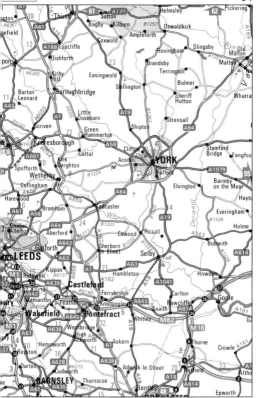

8 km/5 miles

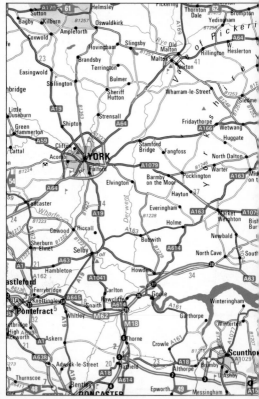

8 km/5 miles

A1039
kton
Filey
Muston
Hunmanby
Reighton
s
North Burton
Bempton
B1229
A165
Flamborough
B1255 B1229 *Flamborough Hd.*
Rudston
Bridlington
Carnaby
Hilderthorpe
A166
Burton
Agnes
Bridlington
Nafferton
Driffield
Bay
Skipsea
B1249
N. Frodingham
Atwick
wick
A165
Brandesburton
Hornsea
30
Leven
B1244
B1243
Long Riston
Mappleton
verley
A1035
Aldbrough
Sproatley
B1238
B1240
Roos
Cottingham
A165
B1235
Withernsea
Anlaby
HULL
Hedon
B1362
New Holland
Ottringham
A1033
Barrow
Patrington
Thornton
Curtis
A1077
A160
Easington
Ulceby
Immingham
Kilnsea
5
A18
B1210
A180
GRIMSBY
A18
Cleethorpes
A18 Scartho
Laceby
50
Humberston

Holderness

Humber

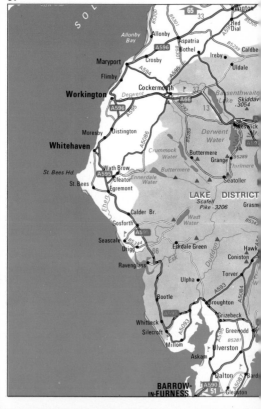

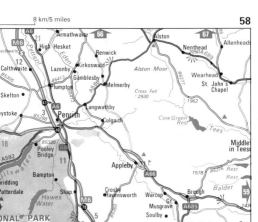

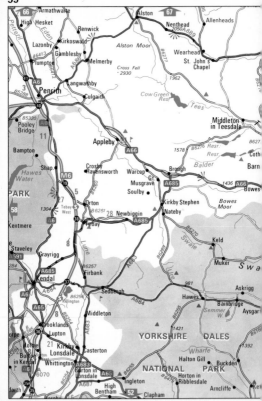

8 km/5 miles

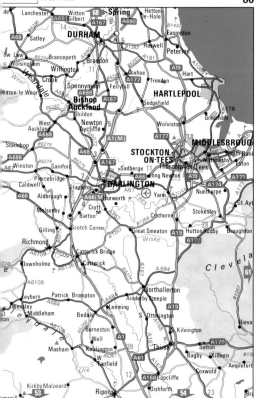

Lanchester A691 Gilbert 68 Spring A690 Hetton-le-Hole Easington

DURHAM B1283 Haswell Peterlee

Satley A167 6 Coxhoe A181

Brancepeth Brandon 11 B6291 Trimdon Hart

Wolsingham Willington Spennymoor A167 Ferryhill HARTLEPOOL

Crook Byers A688 Sedgefield Greatham 178

Witton-le-Wear Weardale Bishop Auckland Shildon Wolviston

West Auckland A688 Newton Aycliffe 5 A177

Staindrop A688 A1(M) STOCKTON-ON-TEES MIDDLESBROUGH South Bank Eston

B6279 A167 7 3 Thornaby-on-Tees A174 A171

Winston B6274 Gainford A167 Sadberge 11 Long Newton A19

Piercebridge Staplton DARLINGTON A66 Yarm

Caldwell A66 A66(M) Hurworth A67 Nunthorpe Gt. Ayt

Aldbrough Croft Crathorne Stokesley

Melsonby Barton Hutton Rudby Broughton

Gilling Scotch Corner Great Smeaton A19 A172 28

Richmond A6108 Catterick Bridge Wiske Cleveland 61

Downholme A6136 Catterick A684 B1257

A6108 A167 A684 Northallerton

Leyburn Patrick Brompton Ainderby Steeple A19

Wensley Middleham A684 Leeming S. Otterington Rieva

Bedale Kilvington A170

Burneston Sutton Kilburn B12

Masham Well Kirklington Bagby Ampleforth

W. Tanfield A61 Thirsk A19 Coxwold

Kirkby Malzeard Ure A168 Topcliffe Dishforth 23

53 Ripon 54

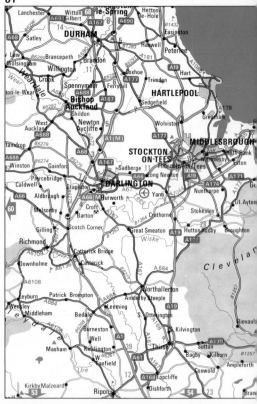

urn
Brotton
Loftus   Staithes
idale
Hinderwell
B1266
B1360   Runswick Bay
A174
31   Lythe   Esk   Whitby
A171
Danby   Egton   Sleights   High Hawsker
stleton   930   Robin Hood's Bay
            Goathland   Ravenscar
ORK MOORS   20
                            Derwent   A171
AL PARK
 ● Rosedale
   Abbey
 ● Lastingham   Cloughton   Burniston
rside   Middleton   Scalby   **Scarborough**
 0   Sinnington   A170
       Pickering   Allerston   A165
            Thornton   Brompton Wykeham   Seamer   Cayton
            Dale   B1415   A64   Folkton   18   Filey
              Yedingham   B1261   Muston   A1039
            B1258   Staxton   A1039   Hunmanby
      Rye Old   Ganton   Reighton
ngsby   Malton   of P i c k e r i n g   Sherburn   W o l d s   A165
    55   Malton   Rillington   Heslerton   Foxholes   North Burton   Bempto
            41   **56**   A165

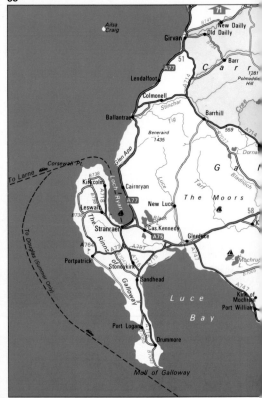

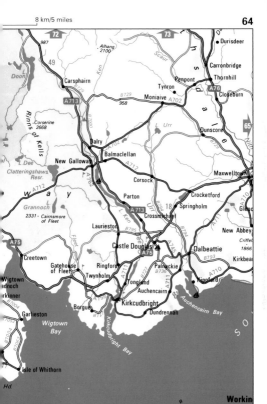

Durisdeer

Carronbridge

Thornhill

Penpont

Closeburn

A76

Moniaive

A702

Tynron

958

Dunscore

65

L.Urr

Maxwelltown

Carsphairn

Alhang
2100

Scaur

987

72

73

Doon

49

A713

B729

Corserine
2668

Rinns of Kells

L.Dee

Clatteringshaws
Resr.

New Galloway

Dalry

Balmaclellan

A712

A762

A713

Corsock

Parton

Crocketford

Springholm

B794

w   a   y

Grannoch

2331 · Cairnsmore
of Fleet

Laurieston

L.Ken

Crossmichael

Castle Douglas

A75

A713

B795

A710

Gleno

New Abbey

Criffel
1866

Dalbeattie

Kirkbea

B793

Creetown

Gatehouse
of Fleet

Ringford

Twynholm

Palnackie

Auchencairn

Kirkcudbright

Dundrennan

Auchencairn Bay

Borgue

Tongland

A711

B736

Nipford

A75

A745

Kirkcudbright Bay

Wigtown
dnoch
rkinner

A75

B7004

Garlieston

Wigtown
Bay

Isle of Whithorn

Hd.

So

Workin

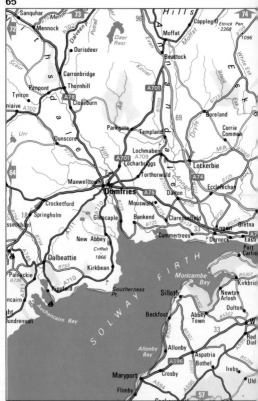

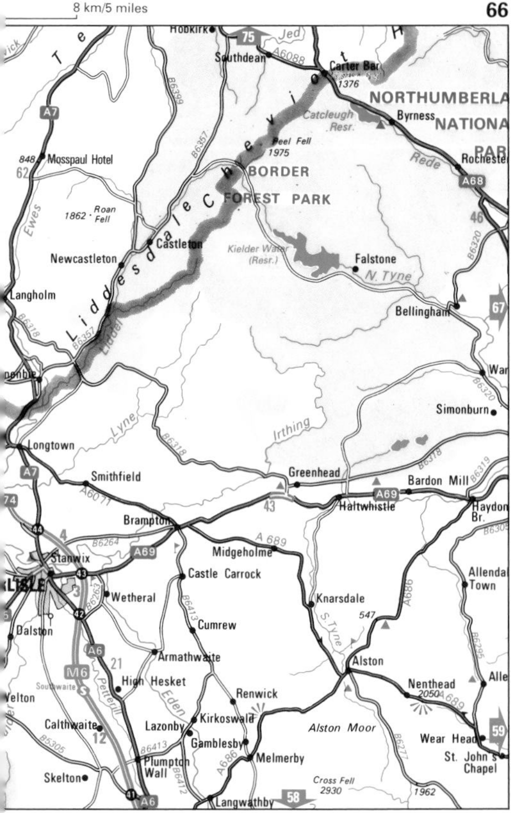

8 km/5 miles

Hobkirk
Jed
Southdean
Carter Bar 1376
NORTHUMBERLA
Catcleugh Resr.
Byrness
NATIONA
A7
Peel Fell 1975
Rochester
848 Mosspaul Hotel
62
Rede
A68
BORDER
FOREST PARK
Roan Fell 1862
46
Ewes
Newcastleton
Castleton
Kielder Water (Resr.)
Falstone
N. Tyne
Langholm
Liddesdale
Bellingham
67
nible
War
Simonburn
Lyne
Irthing
Longtown
A7
Smithfield
Greenhead
Bardon Mill
74
43
Haltwhistle
Haydon Br.
Brampton
A69
44
Stanwix
A689
Midgeholme
Allendal Town
LISLE
3
A69
Wetheral
Castle Carrock
42
5
Dalston
A6
21
Cumrew
Knarsdale
547
Allendal
Armathwaite
S. Tyne
High Hesket
Renwick
Alston
Welton
Lazonby
Kirkoswald
Nenthead 2050
Alle
Calthwaite
12
Gamblesby
Alston Moor
Wear Head
59
St. John's Chapel
Skelton
Plumpton Wall
Melmerby
Cross Fell 2930
1962
A6
Langwathby
58

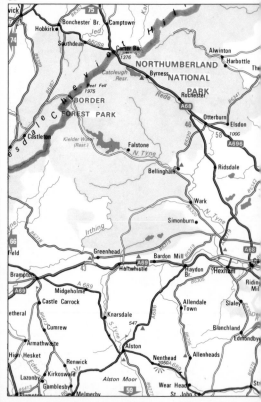

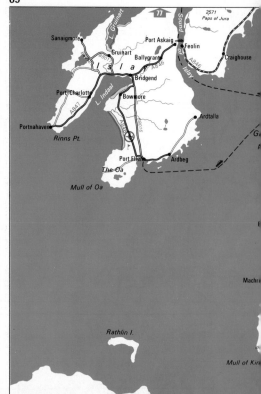

Paps of Jura
2571

Sanaigmore

Port Askaig

Feolin

Gruinart

Ballygrant

Craighouse

Islay

Bridgend

Port Charlotte

Bowmore

L. Indaal

Portnahaven

Ardtalla

Rinns Pt.

Port Ellen

Ardbeg

The Oa

Mull of Oa

Machri

Rathlin I.

Mull of Kin

8 km/5 miles

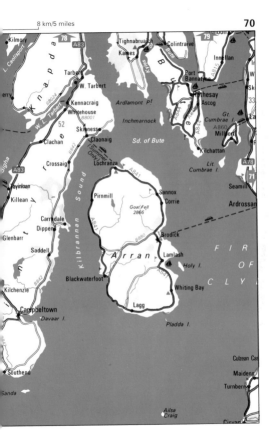

Kilmory

L. Caolisport

K n a p d a

A83

78

Tighnabruaich

Colintraive

79

Kames

B u t e

Innellan

W

erry

Tarbert

W. Tarbert

B8024

Port Bannatyne

W.L. Tarbert

Kennacraig

Ardlamont Pt.

Rothesay

Ascog

Ski

Whitehouse

B8001

Inchmarnock

Gt. Cumbrae I.

A886

33

52

Clachan

Skipness

Millport

Claonaig

Sd. of Bute

B8000

Crossaig

Summer
Only

Kilchattan

A78

Tayinloan

Lochranza

A841

Lit.
Cumbrae I.

71

Killean

K i l b r a n n a n   S o u n d

Pirnmill

Sannox
Corrie

Seamill

Goat Fell
2866

Ardrossan

Carradale

Dippen

B880

Brodick

F I R

Glenbarr

Saddell

A r r a n

Lamlash

Holy I.

O F

Kilchenzie

A841

Blackwaterfoot

C L Y

Whiting Bay

Campbeltown

Lagg

Davaar I.

Pladda I.

Southend

Sanda

Culzean Cas

Maidens

Turnberry

Ailsa
Craig

Cirvan

78

A83

78

Tighnabruaich
Kames
Colintraive

79

Innellan

A770
Port

GR

A78

Tarbert

W. Tarbert

Kennacraig
Whitehouse
B8001

Skipness

Claonaig

Crossaig

Kyles of Bute

B Bute

Port
Bannatyne

Rothesay

Ascog

Ardlamont Pt.

Inchmarnock

A844

A844

Inverkip
Wemyss Bay
Skelmorlie

Gt.
Cumbrae I.

A860
Millport

33

Largs

Lochw

52

Sd. of Bute

Kilchattan

Lit.
Cumbrae I.

Fairlie

A78

Kilbirn

Dalry

A737

Achan

Lochranza

Summer
Only

A841

Pirnmill

Goat Fell
2866

Sannox
Corrie

Seamill

W. Kilbride

Kilwinning

Ardrossan

Steven

Saltcoats

Kilbrannan Sound

A841

A70

B880

Brodick

Arran

Lamlash

Holy I.

FIRTH

Irvine
Bay

Troon

ndale
en

Blackwaterfoot

A841

Whiting Bay

OF

CLYDE

Pres

Lagg

AY

aar I.

own

Pladda I.

A719

Culzean Castle

Maidens
Turnberry

Maybole

Kirkoswald

Ailsa
Craig

New Dailly
Old Dailly

B741

6

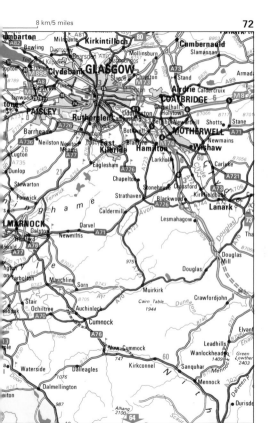

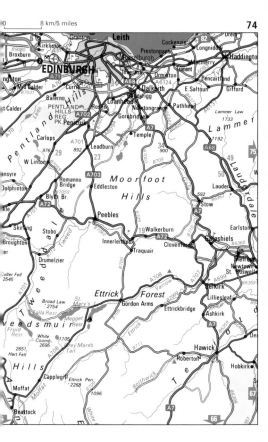

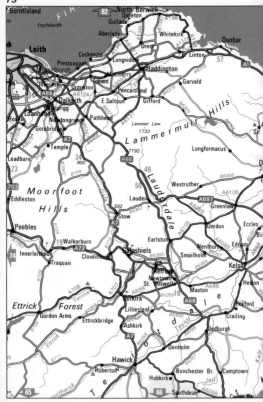

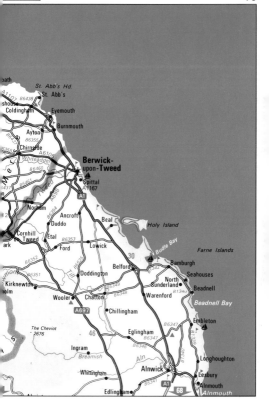

St. Abb's Hd.
ath
B6438 St. Abb's
shouse
Coldingham • Eyemouth
A10?
Ayton • Burnmouth
B6355
Chirnside A6105
B461 **Berwick-**
upon-Tweed
B6460 Spittal
A1167
Norham A1
Ancroft
Duddo Beal
Cornhill Etal B6353 Holy Island
on Tweed Ford Lowick
ark B6352 30 Budle Bay Farne Islands
Belford
Kirknewton B6351 Bamburgh
olm Doddington B6349 North Seahouses
Wooler Chatton B6348 Sunderland Beadnell
A697 Warenford B1340
Chillingham *Beadnell Bay*
B6347
The Cheviot Eglingham
2676 B6347
Ingram 46 Embleton
Breamish Aln
Longhoughton
Whittingham **Alnwick** Lesbury
S A1 Alnmouth
Edlingham 68 *Alnmouth*

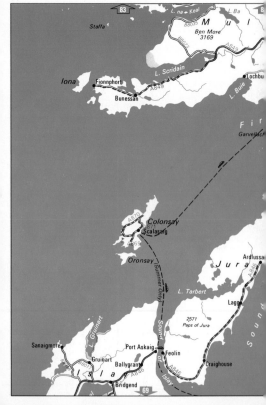

L. na · Keal
L. Ba

Staffa

M u l l

B8035

Ben More
3169

B8035

A849

L. Scridain

Iona Fionnphort

Lochbu

Bunessan

A849

L. Buie

F i r

Garvellach

A870

Colonsay

A871

Scalasaig

A869

Oronsay

Ardlussa

A846

J u r a

L. Tarbert

Lagg

2571
Paps of Jura

S o u n d

Summer Only

Sanaigmore

L. Gruinart

Port Askaig Feolin

Craighouse

Gruinart

Ballygrant

B8017

A846

I s l a

A846

Bridgend

S o u n d   o f   I s l a y

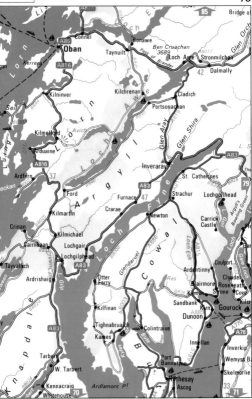

Bridge of

85

Connel
Bonawe
Oban
Taynuilt
Kerrera
Ben Cruachan
3689
Loch Awe
Stronmilchan
Glen Orch
Pass of Brander
42
Dalmally

Kilninver
Kilchrenan
Cladich
Portsonachan

Seil
ile
Loch Avich
Kilmelford

Arduaine
Glen Aray
Glen Shira

Ardfern
37
Inveraray

reckan
Ford
A83
St. Catherines
79

Crinan
Kilmartin
Furnace
47
Strachur
Lochgoilhead

Cairnbaan
Crarae
Newton
Carrick
Castle

Tayvallich
Kilmichael
Lochgair
Lochgilphead
A83

Ardrishaig
Otter
Ferry
Res
Ardentinny
Coulport
Clynder
Blairmore
Rosneath
Cove
Strone

Crinan
Kilfinan
Sandbank
Gourock

swen
Tighnabruaich
Colintraive
Dunoon

Tarbert
Kames
Innellan
Inverkip
Wemyss Ba

W. Tarbert
Port
Bannatyne
Skelmorlie

Kennacraig
Ardlamont Pt
Rothesay
33
71

Whitehouse
Ascog

70

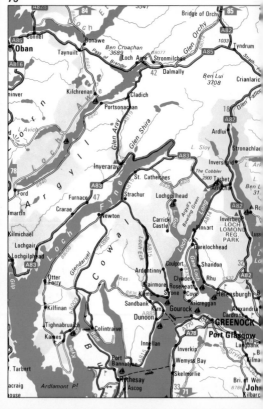

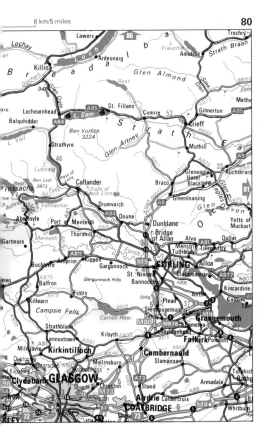

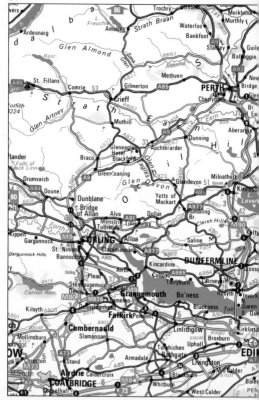

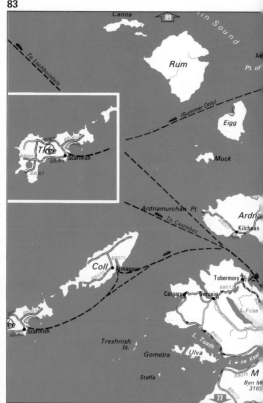

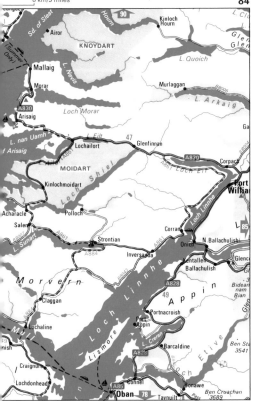

8 km/5 miles

Sd. of Sleat

Airor

90

Kinloch
Hourn

L. Clu

Glen
Glen

KNOYDART

Mallaig

L. Nevis

L. Quoich

Morar

Murlaggan

L. Arkaig

Loch Morar

A830

Arisaig

Ga

L. nan Uamh

L. Eilt

47

Glenfinnan

A830

Corpach

of Arisaig

Lochailort

MOIDART

Loch Shiel

Loch Eil

Fort
Willia

Kinlochmoidart

Acharacle

Polloch

Corran

L.
85

Salen

Strontian

Onich

N. Ballachulish

A884

Inversanda

Kentallen

Glenc

L. Sunart

Ballachulish

A861

Glen

Loch Linnhe

A828

Morvern

Appin

49

3

Bideann
nam
Bian

Claggan

Portnacroish

Glen

Loch Linnhe

Lochaline

Port
Appin

L. Crerar

Ben Sta
3541

A828

Barcaldine

Etive

Mull

Lismore

Craignur

A85

Bonawe

Ben Cruachan
3689

nish

Lochdonhead

Connel

78

Oban

Taynuilt

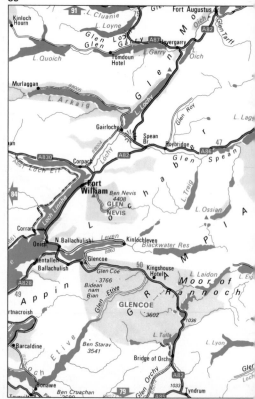

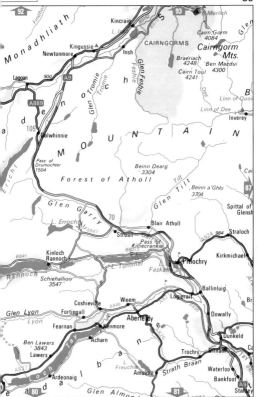

8 km/5 miles

92
93

Findhorn

Monadhliath

Kincraig

B9152

CAIRNGORMS

Morlich

Glen

Cairn Gorm
4084

Cairngorm
Mts.

Kingussie
Newtonmore

Insh

Braeriach
4248

Ben Macdui
4300

Cairn Toul
4241

Dee

Laggan

A9

900

Glen Tromie

Tromie

Glen Feshie

Feshie

Linn of Quoi

Linn of Dee

Inverey

B

A889

Ercht

105

Dalwhinnie

M

O

U

N

e

n

o

T

A

d

a

Pass of
Drumochter
1504

*Beinn Dearg
3304*

I

N

Forest of Atholl

Glen Tilt

Tilt

Beinn a'Glo
3704

87

L. Errochy

Glen Garry

70

B8847

Struan

Blair Atholl

Pass of
Killiecrankie

A924

984

Straloch

Spittal of
Glensh

Kinloch
Rannoch

B8846

Schiehallion
3547

L. Tummel

Faskally

Pitlochry

Kirkmichael

Ballinluig

Ar

Br

Rannoch

Glen Lyon

Lyon

Coshieville

Fortingall

Fearnan

Weem

Aberfeldy

A827

Logierait

Dowally

Dunkeld

Ben Lawers
3843

Lawers

Kenmore

Acharn

L
a

n

L
Freuchie

Trochry

Birnam

Ca

Ardeonaig

80

Loch Tay

a

y

d

l

Amulree

Strath Braan

Waterloo

Bankfoot

A9

Stanley

Glen Almond

Glen Lyon

A827

81

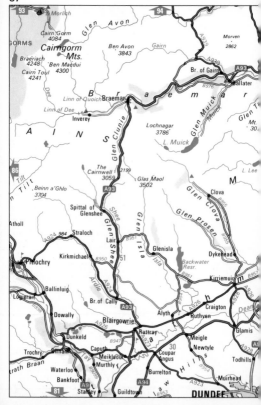

Morlich

93

94

Glen Avon

GORMS

Cairngorm Mts.

Cairn Gorm
4084

Ben Avon
3843

Gairn

Morven
2862

Braeriach
4248

Ben Macdui
4300

A939

Cairn Toul
4241

Dee

Br. of Gairn

A976

A93

Linn of Quoich

Braemar

Ballater

Linn of Dee

Braemar

Glen Muick

Glen Te

Inverey

Lochnagar
3786

L. Muick

Mt.
30

AIN

Glen Clunie

L Lee

86

The Cairnwell
3059

2199

Glas Maol
3502

M

Tilt

Beinn a'Ghlo
3704

Glen Isla

Glen Clova

Clova

A93

Glen Shee

Glen Prosen

Atholl

Spittal of
Glenshee

A924 984

Straloch

Lair

B951

Glenisla

Dykehead

Pitlochry

Kirkmichael

B950

51

Isla

Backwater
Resr.

Kirriemuir

m

A957

Ballinluig

Ardle

A924

Br. of Cally

A926

Craigton

Dear

Logierait

Dowally

A93

Blairgowrie

Alyth

Ruthven

Glamis

A928

Trochry

Dunkeld

A923

A926

Rattray

a

Meigle

Newtyle

Todhills

A9

Strath Braan

Birnam

Caputh

Meikleour

Murthly

Coupar
Angus

30

Burrelton

w

Hills

s

A923

Muirhead

Waterloo

Bankfoot

Stanley

Guildtown

B953

A94

DUNDEE

81

A58

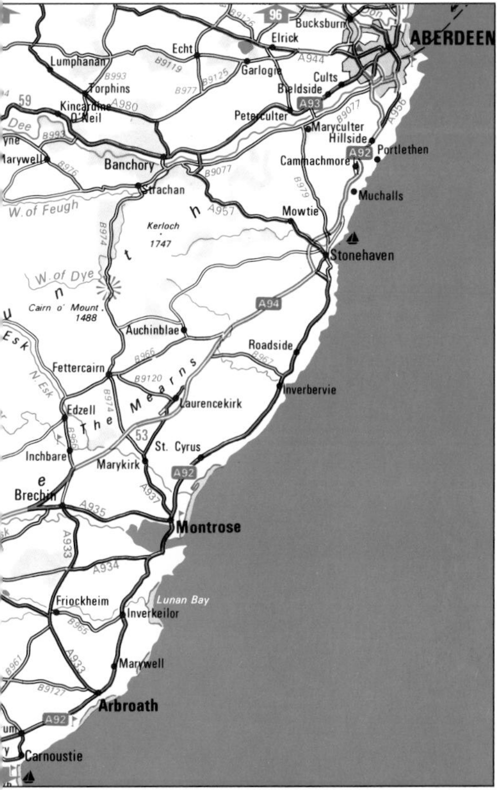

8 km/5 miles

Bucksburn
Echt
Elrick
ABERDEEN
Lumphanan
Torphins
Garlogie
Bieldside
Cults
Kincardine
O'Neil
Peterculter
Maryculter
Hillside
Portlethen
Dee
Banchory
Cammachmore
Strachan
Muchalls
larywell
W. of Feugh
Kerloch
1747
Mowtie
W. of Dye
Stonehaven
Cairn o' Mount
1488
Auchinblae
Roadside
Fettercairn
Esk
Inverbervie
Edzell
Laurencekirk
Inchbare
St. Cyrus
Marykirk
Brechin
Montrose
Friockheim
Lunan Bay
Inverkeilor
Marywell
Arbroath
Carnoustie

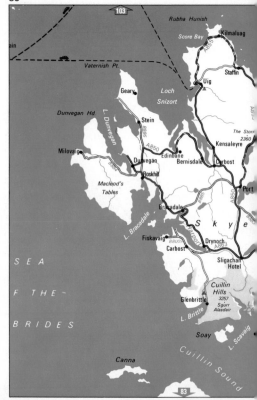

103

Rubha Hunish

Score Bay

Kilmaluag

ain

A855

Staffin

Vaternish Pt.

Uig

A855

Geary

Loch
Snizort

Dunvegan Hd.

Stein

L. Dunvegan

B886

The Storr
2360

A855

Kensaleyre

A850

Milovaig

Edinbane

Bernisdale

Carbost

Dunvegan

Roskhill

A850

Port

Macleod's
Tables

S k y e

Bracadale

L. Bracadale

B8009

A863

A850

Fiskavaig

Drynoch

Carbost

S E A

Sligachan
Hotel

F T H E

Cuillin
Hills
3257
Sgurr
Alasdair

Glenbrittle

B R I D E S

L. Brittle

L. Scavaig

Soay

Cuillin Sound

Canna

83

Poolewe

STRATHNASHEALLAG
Fionn
Loch

97

Gair Loch
Gairloch

Loch Maree

Loch Maree
Hotel

Slioch
3217

LOCH MAREE

Kinlochewe

Achna

Loch Torridon

Diabaig

TORRIDON

Ben Eighe
3309

Inverallign

Upr.
L. Torridon

Torridon
3456

L. a Chro

Rona

Shieldaig

BEN DAMPH

L.
Damh

APPLECROSS

Glen Carron

91

Beinn
Bhan
2936

asay

2054

Applecross

Lochcarron

Achintee

Toscaig

Kishorn

L. Kishorn

L. Carron

Inner Sound

Plockton

Stromeferry
A890

Ling

L. M

pay

Duirinish

Elchaig

Falls of
Glomach

Kyle of Lochalsh
A87

Kyleakin

L. Alsh

Dornie

KINTAIL
Inverinate

Mam Sou
3862

L. A

adford

Breakish

(Summer
Only)

Loch Duich

Ben Attow
3383

Affric

Isle
Oronsay

Kylerhea

Glenelg

Shiel Bridge

Invershiel

A87

Cluanie
889 Br

L. Cl

Teangue

GLENELG

Arnisdale

Loch Hourn

Kinloch
Hourn

Gle

af

Sd. of Sleat

Airor

84

KNOYDART

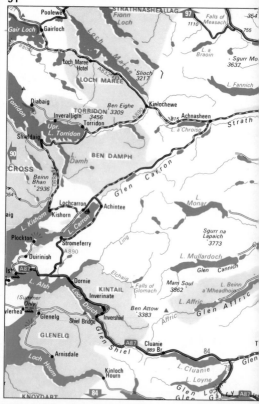

8 km/5 miles

99

trath
aich
esr.

L. Eye

Fearn

L. Morie

Alness

A9

Barbaraville

Nigg B.

Invergordon

Nigg

Cromarty

Ben Wyvis
3249

Evanton

Balblair

MOR

arnoch

61

L. Glass

Garve

L. Garve

Dingwall

Cromarty Firth

61

Strathpeffer

A835

Rosemarkie

Fort
George

Nairn

onan

Contin

A9

Avoch

Fortrose

Ardersier

Marybank

A832

Conon Br

Munlochy

Firth of Inverness

A96

Cawdo

rin

Muir of Ord

Redcastle

N

Kessock

Croy

Orrin
Resr.

Windhill

Beauly

Beauly Firth

Clachnaharry

INVERNESS

93

Kilmorack

Ness

A82

Daviot

A9

Struy

Beauly

Dores

L. Duntelchaig

Meikle

Glass

Moy

Drumnadrochit

Strath Nairn

Glen Urquhart

Torness

Tomatin

46

1189

Inverfarigaig

Loch Ness

Fovers

Errogie

L. Mhor

Strath Errick

nriston

e 66

Aviemore

us 4

A82

Glen Tarff

85

Strath

Dulnain

monadhliath Mountains

86

Kincraig

L. Insh

CAI

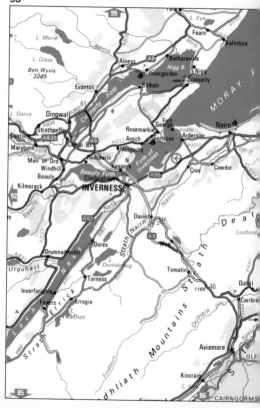

8 km/5 miles

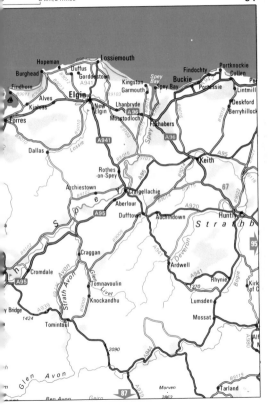

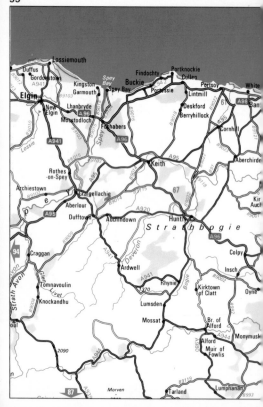

8 km/5 miles

Pennan
Rosehearty
Fraserburgh
Inverallochy
St. Combs
New Aberdour
Rathen
A92
A98
New Pitsligo
Strichen
Crimond
A952
18
Newbyth
Cuminestown
Buchan
Mintlaw
Peterhead
A950
New Deer
Old Deer
A92
Ciola
Burnhaven
43
Methlick
Ythan
A952
Cruden Bay
Cruden Bay
Tarves
Ellon
33
Oldmeldrum
A920
A999
Collieston
A90
Newburgh
Newmachar
A92
Kintore
A96
Dyce
Blackburn
Bucksburn
Elrick
A944
ABERDEEN
Garlogie
Cults

To Lerwick & Stromness

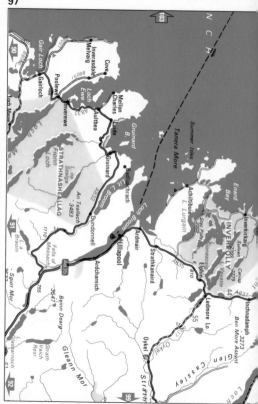

0   8 km/5 miles

Pt. of Stoer

Culkein

Drumbeg

Eddrachillis Bay

Handa

Badcall

Scourie

Laxford Br.

A894

Ben Stack 2364

Kylesku

Arkle 2580

Foinaven

Rhiconich

A838

Dionard

Kinlochbervie

Cape Wrath

The Parbh

Kyle of Durness

Durness

63

Reay Forest

Stack L.

A838

Eriboll

L. Eriboll

100

97

48

93

Strath Oykel

Loch Shin

Altass

Lairg

Oykel

Carron

Invercharron

Inveran

A836

Shin Falls

A838

A839

Ardgay

Kincardine

Bonar Br.

Strath Brora

Block

L. Morie

L. Glass

Alness

A9

Edderton

Spinningdale

Evelix

Easthaven

Tain

A836

A949

Dornoch

Fleet

L. Brora

Pittentrail

Ben Uarie

2046

of Kildonan

Barbaraville

Fearn

L. Eye

Dornoch

Firth

Inver

Dornoch

Golspie

Helmsdale

Kildonan

Balintore

Portmahomack

Tarbat Ness

Brora

Crackaig

Portgower

Helmsdale

A9

76

Berriedale

Hopeman

RTH

0 8 km/5 miles

98

L. Eriboll

Smoo

Eriboll

A838

Ben Hope 3040

741

Hope

Melness

Kinloch

Ben Loyal 2504

Tongue

Skerray

Farr

Armadale

Strathy Pt.

Loch Loyal

Bonigie

Strath Naver

Naver

Bettyhill

A836

Strathy

44

Strathy

Strathy

Portskerra

Melvich

B871

L. nan Cuinne

Loch Baddanloch

L. nan Chair

Altnaharra

Kirtomy

A836

Castle Kirtback 2367

Forsinard Hotel 663

Strath Halladale

Trantlebeg

Golval

Reay

Dounreay

A836

B870

Forss

Calder

Thurso

Strabster

To Stromness

Kinbrace

Dunbeath

Thurso

Halkirk

B874

Myster

Castletown

Roadside

A882

A9

Dunnet

Latheron

A895

Loch Watten

A9

101

Dunbeath

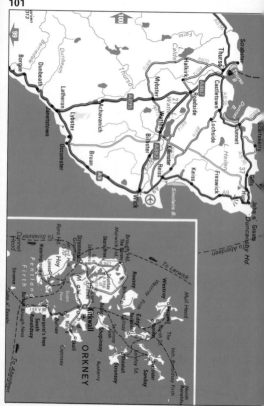

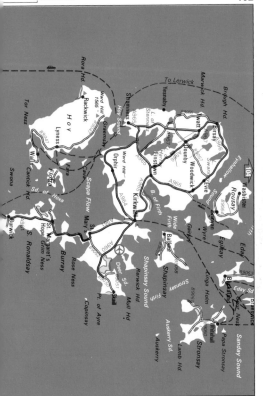

8 km/5 miles

To Lerwick

Rora Hd.

Ward Hill 1565 ▲

Rackwick

H O Y

Lyness

Tor Ness

Wall

Cantick Hd.

Sd. of Hoxa

Swona

Burwick

S. Ronaldsay

Graemsay

Hoy Sound

Stromness

Yesnaby

L. of Stenness

Evie

Marwick Hd.

Birsay

Twatt

Dounby

Finstown

Woodwick

Swannay

Ward Hill

Orphir

B. of Firth

Kirkwall

Scapa Flow

St. Margaret's Hope

Grim Ness

Burray

Rose Ness

Maes

Holm

Deer Sd.

Pt. of Ayre

Copinsay

Widewall

Wide Firth

Carness

Balfour

Shapinsay

Shapinsay Sound

Renwick Hd.

Mull Hd.

Inganess

Gairsay

Wyre

Egilsay

Rousay

Eynhallow Sound

Brough Hd.

Papa Stronsay

Wasbister

Eday

Calf of Eday

Eday Sd.

Auskerry Sd.

Auskerry

Stronsay Firth

Stronsay

Lamb Hd.

Whitehall

Sanday Sound

To Lerwick

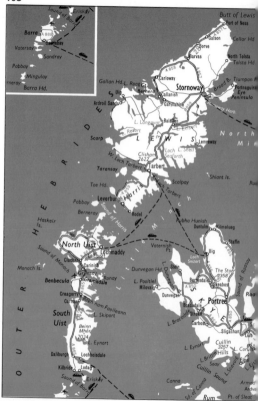

30 km/20 miles

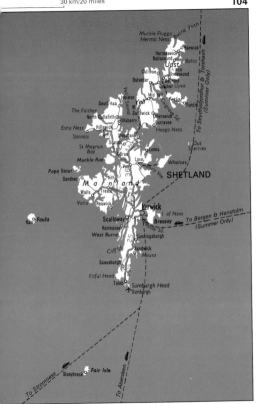

Muckle Flugga
Herma Ness
Harold swick
Unst
Baltasound
Balta
Dullhoe
Uyeasound
Belmont
Haroldswick
Dalseter
Mid Yell
Fetlar
Lobister
Yell
Funzie
South-haa
W.
Sandwick
North Collafirth
Ollaberry
Otterswick
Burravoe
The Faither
Esha Ness
Hillswick
Heoga Ness
Stenness
Voxter
St Magnus
Bay
Scatsta
Muckle Roe
Brae
Lunna
Out
Skerries
Papa Stour
Voe
Whalsay
Sandness
Aith
SHETLAND
Mainland
Laxo
Yell Sound
Walls
Tresta
Vaila
Reawick
I. of Noss
Lerwick
Bressay
To Bergen & Hanstolm
(Summer Only)
Scalloway
Hamnavoe
West Burra
Gulberwick
Cliff
Sandwick
Scousburgh
Mousa
Fitful Head
Tolob
Sumburgh Head
Sumburgh

Hascosay
Foula

To Stromness
Stonybreck
Fair Isle

To Aberdeen

To Scalloway/Toft/Ulsta/Torshavn
(Summer Only)

105 Index

The reference number refers to the page, and the letter refers to the section of the map in which the index entry can be found, as divided into **a**, **b**, **c**, and **d** thus:

Alresford	10a	Ardfern	78a
Alrewas	36a	Ardgay	99c
Alston	66d	Ardlui	79b
Alston Cross	28c	Ardlussa	77d
Altassmore	99b	Ardmair	97b
Altnaharra	100a	Ardminish	70a
Alton	10b	Ardrishaig	78c
Altrincham	46b	Ardrossan	71b
Alva	81c	Ardtalla	69b
Alvanley	46c	Arduaine	78a
Alvaston	36b	Arinagour	83c
Alvechurch	28a	Arisaig	84a
Alyth	87d	Armadale (Skye)	84a
Amble	68a	Armadale (Highland)	100b
Ambleside	58c	Arncliffe	52b
Amersham	18a	Arnesby	37c
Amesbury	9b	Arnisdale	90d
Amlwch	43b	Arnprior	80c
Ammanford	23b	Arnside	51b
Ampleforth	61d	Arrochar	79d
Ampthill	30c	Arthog	33a
Amulree	80b	Arundel	11c
Ancaster	38a	Ascot	18c
Ancroft	76c	Asfordby	37b
Andover	9b	Ash	14a
Andoversford	28c	Ashbourne	36a
Annan	65d	Ashburton	4a
Annbank	72c	Ashby	49b
Anstruther	82b	Ashby de la Zouch	36b
Appleby	58b	Ashford (Kent)	13b
Applecross	90a	Ashington	68a
Appledore (Devon)	5b	Ashstead	19c
Appledore (Kent)	13d	Ashton Keynes	16b
Arbroath	88c	Ashton-under-Lyne	47a
Archiestown	94a	Ashton-in-Makerfield	46a
Ardarroch	90c	Askham	57d
Ardbeg	69b	Aspatria	65d
Ardcharnich	97c	Aston	48a
Ardentinny	79d	Atherstone	36d
Ardeonaig	80a	Atherton	46a
Ardersier	93b	Attleborough	42a

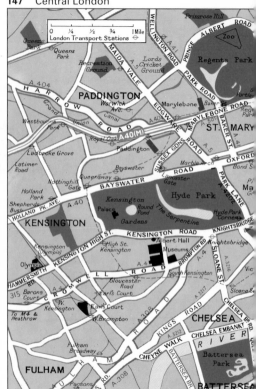

London Transport Stations ⊖

0 ¼ ½ ¾ 1 Mile

Primrose Hill

Zoo

Queens Park

Queens Park

Recreation Ground

Lords Cricket Ground

Regents Park

A 404

MAIDA VALE

PADDINGTON

Marylebone

Baker St

St. MARY

HARROW ROAD

Warwick Ave.

EDGWARE

MARYLEBONE ROAD

BAKER ST.

OXFORD

Grand Union Canal

Royal Oak A40(M)

Paddington

Marble Arch

Bond St.

Ladbroke Grove

Latimer Road

Westbourne Park

Bayswater

Sussex Gdns.

Lancaster Gate

PARK LANE

Hyde Park Corner

Westbourne Road

Queensway

BAYSWATER

Nottinghill Gate

ROAD

Holland Park

Shepherds Bush

HOLLAND PK. AVE.

A 40

Kensington Palace

Round Pond

Gardens

Hyde Park

The Serpentine

Hyde Park Corner

KENSINGTON

Kensington (Olympia)

KENSINGTON HIGH ST.

High St. Kensington

KENSINGTON ROAD

Albert Hall

Museums

KNIGHTSBRIDGE

Knightsbridge

SLOANE ST.

Vic

Olympia

HAMMERSMITH RD.

315

Barons Court

CROMWELL

Gloucester Road

BROMPTON RD.

South Kensington

A 4

ROAD

W. Kensington

Earls Court

Earl's Court

KINGS

CHELSEA

Chelsea

Sloane Sq

To M4 & Heathrow

W. Brompton

ROAD

A 3217

A 3220

CHELSEA BR RD

Fulham Broadway

FULHAM RD.

CHEYNE WALK

CHELSEA EMBANKT.

RIVER

Battersea Park

FULHAM

Parsons Green

FULHAM RD.

A 308

BATTERSEA BR.

BATTERSEA

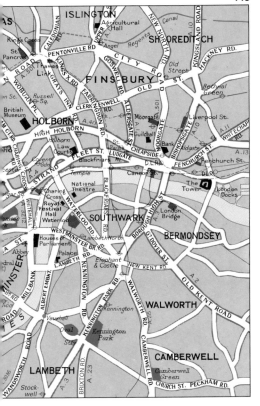

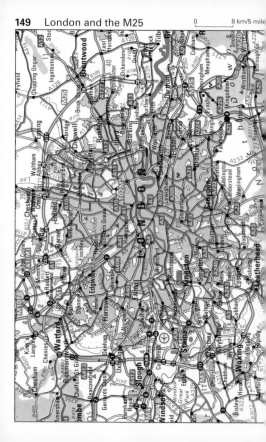

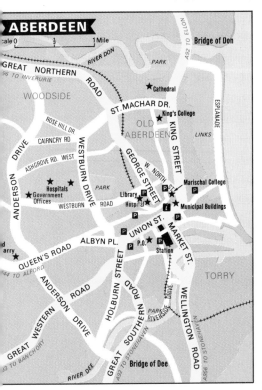

ABERDEEN

Scale 0   ½   1 Mile

TO ELLON

Bridge of Don

A492

RIVER DON

GREAT NORTHERN ROAD

A96 TO INVERURIE

PARK

WOODSIDE

★ Cathedral

ST. MACHAR DR.

ROSE HILL DR

King's College ★

OLD ABERDEEN

CAIRNCRY RD

ESPLANADE

ASHGROVE RD. WEST

WESTBURN DRIVE

KING STREET

GEORGE STREET

LINKS

ANDERSON DRIVE

PARK

W. NORTH ST.

Marischal College ★

★ Hospitals
★ Government
Offices

Library ★

P

P

WESTBURN ROAD

Hospital ★

i

★ Municipal Buildings

P

d
arry

UNION ST.

P

P

MARKET ST.

ALBYN PL.

P.O. ★

A944 TO ALFORD

QUEEN'S ROAD

Station

TORRY

ANDERSON ROAD

HOLBURN STREET

SOUTHERN ROAD

WELLINGTON ROAD

A92 TO STONEHAVEN

RIVERSIDE DRIVE

A956 TO NIGG

PARK

GREAT WESTERN ROAD

A93 TO BANCHORY

GREAT SOUTHERN ROAD

RIVER DEE

A92 TO STONEHAVEN

Bridge of Dee

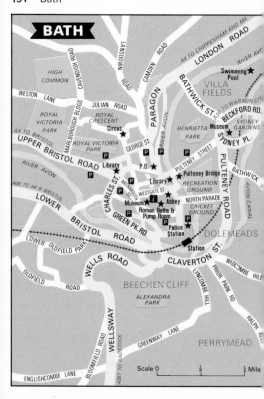

BATH

HIGH COMMON

WESTON LANE

CAVENDISH ROAD

LANSDOWN

CAMDEN ROAD

PARAGON

A4 TO CHIPPENHAM AND M4

LONDON ROAD

RIVER AVON

Swimming Pool ★

VILLA FIELDS

BATHWICK ST

A36 TO WARMINSTER

BECKFORD RD.

SYDNEY GARDENS

JULIAN ROAD

ROYAL CRESCENT

MARLBOROUGH BLDGS

ROYAL VICTORIA PARK

Circus ★

GEORGE ST.

RIVER AVON

HENRIETTA PARK

Museum ★

SYDNEY PL.

A4 TO BRISTOL

UPPER BRISTOL ROAD

ROYAL VICTORIA PARK

P

P

P

P

PULTENEY STREET

BATHWICK

Library ★

P.O. ★

Library ★

Pulteney Bridge ★

PULTENEY ROAD

AVON CANAL

RIVER AVON

CHARLES ST.

MINMOUTH ST.

WESTGATE ST.

RECREATION GROUND

LOWER

BRISTOL ROAD

GREEN PK. RD.

Museum ★

Abbey ★

Roman Baths & Pump Room ★

NORTH PARADE

CRICKET GROUND

Police Station ★

DOLEMEADS

A36 TO A4 & BRISTOL

LOWER OLDFIELD PARK

Station ■

CLAVERTON ST.

WELLS ROAD

OLDFIELD ROAD

BEECHEN CLIFF

ALEXANDRA PARK

LYNCOMBE HILL

PRIOR PARK RD.

WIDCOMBE HILL

RALPH RD.

WELLSWAY

BLOOMFIELD ROAD

GREENWAY LANE

PERRYMEAD

ENGLISHCOMBE LANE

A367 TO RADSTOCK

Scale 0   ¼   ½ Mile

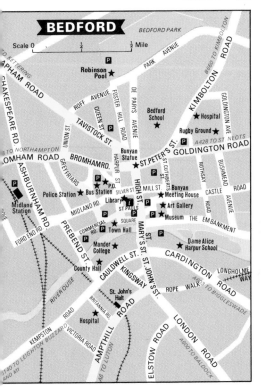

BEDFORD

BEDFORD PARK

Scale 0   ¼   ½ Mile

Robinson Pool ★

PARK AVENUE

CLAPHAM ROAD

SHAKESPEARE RD

TO KETTERING

ROFF AVENUE

FOSTER HILL ROAD

DE PARYS AVENUE

QUEEN ST

UNION ST

TAVISTOCK ST

Bedford School ★

KIMBOLTON

8660 TO KIMBOLTON

GOLDINGTON RD

Hospital ★

GOLDINGTON AVE

Rugby Ground ★

TO NORTHAMPTON

CLOMHAM ROAD

BROMHAM RD.

HARPUR ST

GREYFRIARS

Bunyan Statue ★

★ST.PETER'S ST.

ST CUTHBERT'S ST

A428 TO ST NEOTS

GOLDINGTON ROAD

ROTHSAY

BUSHMEAD

CASTLE

ROAD

AVENUE

Police Station ★ Bus Station

★ P.O.

HIGH ST

MILL ST

SILVER ST

★ Bunyan Meeting House

Library ★

MIDLAND RD.

ST PAULS

SQUARE

★ Art Gallery

★ Museum

THE EMBANKMENT

ASHBURNHAM RD

Midland Station

FORD END RD

PREBEND ST.

COMMERCIAL RD.

Town Hall

MARY'S ST.

Mander College ★

County Hall

CAULDWELL ST.

KINGSWAY

ST. JOHN'S ST.

Dame Alice Harpur School ★

CARDINGTON ROAD

LONGHOLME WAY

A603 TO BIGGLESWADE

RIVER OUSE

BRITANNIA RD.

St. John's Halt ★

Hospital ★

KEMPSTON

A5140 TO LEIGHTON BUZZARD AND M1

ROAD

VICTORIA ROAD

AMPTHILL

ROAD

ROPE WALK

ELSTOW ROAD

LONDON ROAD

A6 TO LUTON

A600 TO BALDOCK

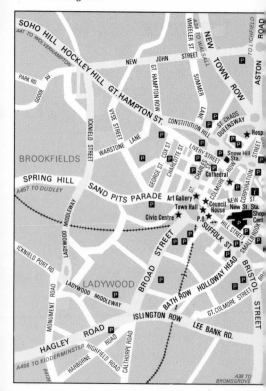

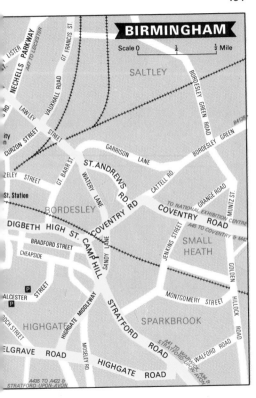

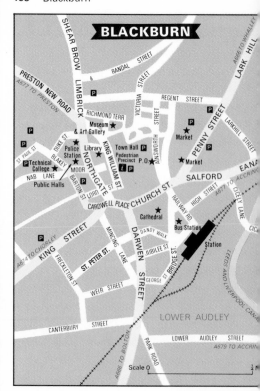

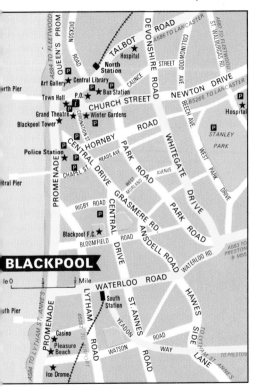

BLACKPOOL

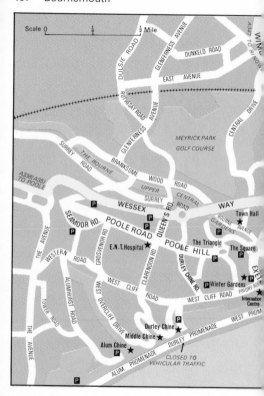

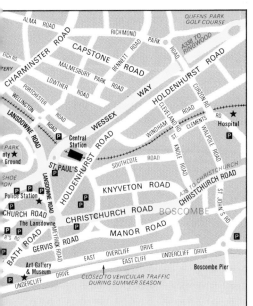

BOURNEMOUTH

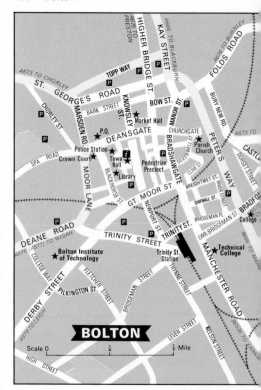

BOLTON

Scale 0 — ¼ — ½ Mile

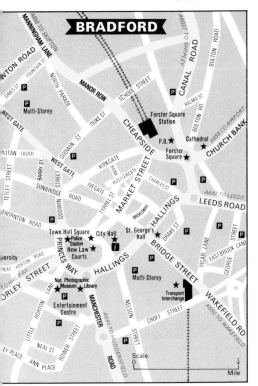

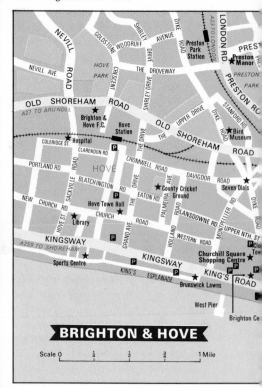

BRIGHTON & HOVE

Scale 0   ¼   ½   ¾   1 Mile

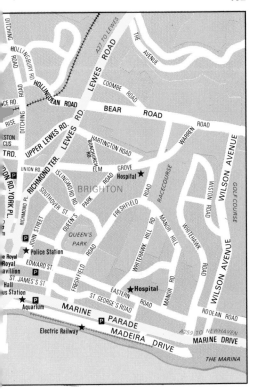

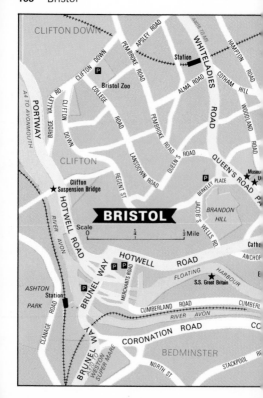

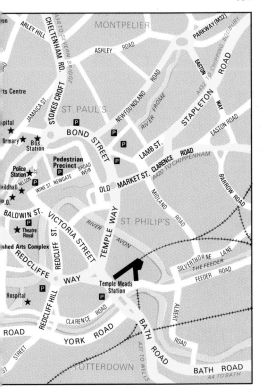

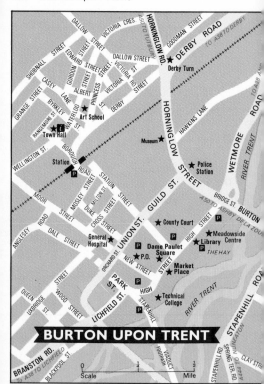

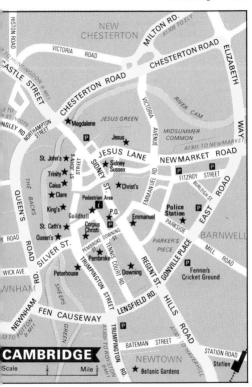

HISTON ROAD

NEW CHESTERTON

MILTON RD.

A1309 TO ELY

VICTORIA ROAD

CHESTERTON ROAD

ELIZABETH

CASTLE STREET

TO HUNTINGDON & M11

CHESTERTON ROAD

NORTHAMPTON STREET

3 TO ST. NEOTS

NGLEY RD.

RIVER CAM

VICTORIA AVENUE

JESUS GREEN

MIDSUMMER COMMON

WAY

★ Magdalene

P

Jesus ★

A1303 TO NEWMARKET

JESUS LANE

NEWMARKET ROAD

ST. JOHN'S STREET

SIDNEY ST.

Sidney Sussex

P

St. John's ★

Trinity ★

FITZROY STREET

BURLEIGH ST.

EAST ROAD

Caius ★

★ Christ's

THE BACKS

Clare ★

EMMANUEL RD.

Police Station

King's ★

i

Pedestrian Area

Guildhall

P.O.

Emmanuel

PARKSIDE

BARNWELL

St. Cath's ★

Corpus Christi

P

QUEEN'S

ROAD

Queen's ★

PEMBROKE

DOWNING ST.

PARKER'S PIECE

MILL ROAD

ROAD

TENNIS COURT RD.

Pembroke

GONVILLE PLACE

REGENT ST.

Downing

Fenner's Cricket Ground

Peterhouse

TRUMPINGTON STREET

WICK AVE.

SILVER ST.

NWHAM

SHEEPS GREEN

FEN CAUSEWAY

NEWNHAM

13 TO POTTON & M11

LENSFIELD RD.

HILLS ROAD

A1309 TO ROYSTON & M11

TRUMPINGTON RD.

BATEMAN STREET

A604 TO HAVERHILL

STATION ROAD

Station

CAMBRIDGE

Scale ¼ Mile ½

NEWTOWN

★ Botanic Gardens

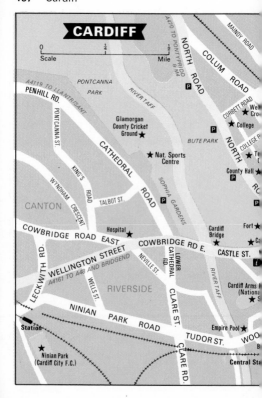

CARDIFF

Scale
0 — ¼ — Mile

A470 TO PONTYPRIDD 8 M4

MAINDY ROAD

COLUM ROAD

NORTH ROAD

A4119 TO LLANTRISANT

PENHILL RD.

PONTCANNA PARK

RIVER TAFF

CORBETT ROAD
★ Wel
★ Cro
College

PONTCANNA ST.

Glamorgan County Cricket Ground ★

BUTE PARK

NORTH RD.

COLLEGE R

★ College

CATHEDRAL ROAD

★ Nat. Sports Centre

KING'S ROAD

★ Te
C

County Hall ★

WYNDHAM CRESCENT

TALBOT ST.

SOPHIA GARDENS

RO

CANTON

COWBRIDGE ROAD

Hospital ★

COWBRIDGE RD E.

Cardiff Bridge

Fort ★

★ Ca

CASTLE ST.

LECKWITH RD.

WELLINGTON STREET

A4161 TO A48 AND BRIDGEND

CATHEDRAL RD.

LOWER

NEVILLE ST.

RIVERSIDE

WELLS ST.

NINIAN PARK ROAD

CLARE ST.

RIVER TAFF

Cardiff Arms
(National
★ S

Station

Empire Pool ★

TUDOR ST.

WOO

B

★ Ninian Park (Cardiff City F.C.)

CLARE RD.

Central Sta

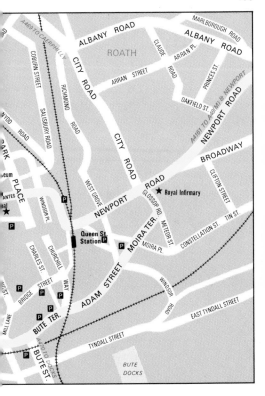

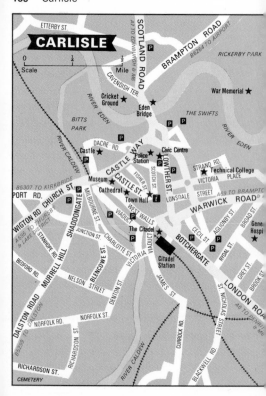

CARLISLE

ETTERBY ST.

SCOTLAND ROAD

BRAMPTON ROAD

B6264 TO AIRPORT

A9 TO EDINBURGH & M6

CAVENDISH TER.

RICKERBY PARK

0 — ¼ — ½ Mile
Scale

War Memorial ★

Cricket Ground ★

RIVER EDEN

Eden Bridge ★

THE SWIFTS

BITTS PARK

RIVER EDEN

RIVER CALDEW

DACRE RD.

CASTLE WAY

Castle ★

Civic Centre ★

B5307 TO KIRKBRIDE

Police Station ★

STRAND RD.

Museum ★

CASTLE ST.

FISHER ST.

SCOTCH ST.

LOWTHER ST.

Technical College ★
PLACE

VICTORIA

PORT RD.

Cathedral ★

Town Hall ★ i

LONSDALE

STREET

A69 TO BRAMPTO

WARWICK ROAD

WEST WALLS

WIGTON RD.

CHURCH ST.

SHADDONGATE

MILBOURNE ST.

VIADUCT

CECIL ST.

AGLIONBY ST.

Gene
Hospi ★

A595 TO THURS & LAKE DISTRICT

A686 TO

The Citadel ★

VICTORIA

BOTCHERGATE

BROAD ST.

MURRELL HILL

JUNCTION ST.

CHARLOTTE ST.

RYDAL ST.

STANWIX RD.

BEDFORD RD.

BLENCOWE ST.

Citadel Station ★

LONDON ROAD

GREY ST.

NELSON STREET

DENTON ST.

JAMES ST.

ST. NICHOLAS STREET

A6 TO PENRI

DALSTON ROAD

B5299 TO DALSTON

NORFOLK RD.

NORFOLK ST.

RIVER CALDEW

CURROCK RD.

BLACKWELL RD.

RICHARDSON ST.

RICHARDSON ST.

CEMETERY

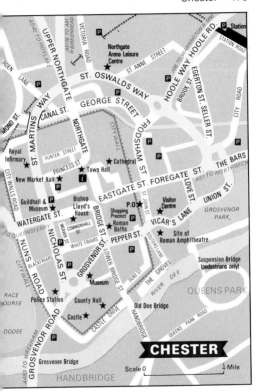

CHESTER

Scale 0 ____ ¼ Mile

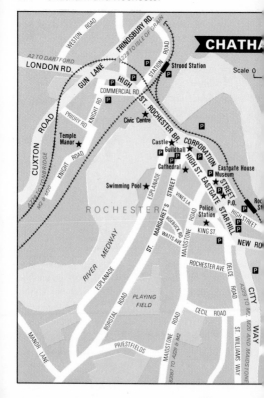

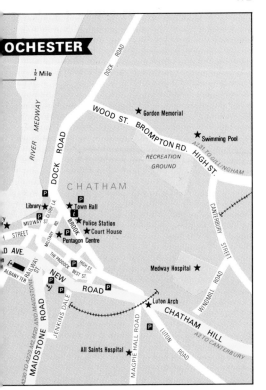

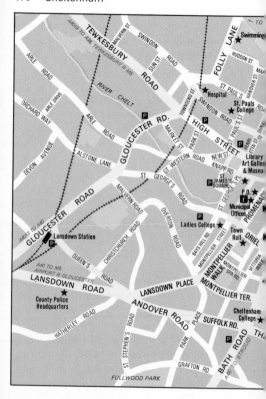

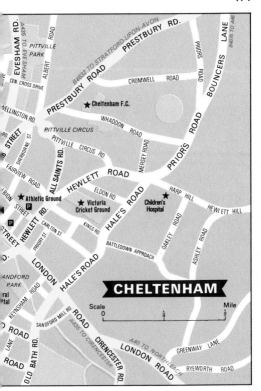

CHELTENHAM

Scale
0   ¼   Mile

EVESHAM RD.
B4632 TO EVESHAM
PITTVILLE PARK
ALBERT ROAD
ROAD
CEN. CROSS DRIVE
B4632 TO STRATFORD-UPON-AVON
PRESTBURY RD.
PRESTBURY ROAD
CROMWELL ROAD
PRIORS ROAD
BOUNCERS LANE
B4075 TO A46
WELLINGTON RD.
★ Cheltenham F.C.
WHADDON ROAD
STREET
SHERBORNE ST.
PITTVILLE CIRCUS
PITTVILLE CIRCUS RD.
FAIRVIEW ROAD.
ALL SAINTS RD.
HEWLETT ROAD
MEISEY ROAD
PRIORS ROAD
HARP HILL
HEWLETT HILL
★ Athletic Ground
ALBION STREET
ELDON RD.
★ Victoria Cricket Ground
HALE'S ROAD
Children's Hospital
OAKLEY ROAD
ASHLEY ROAD
HEWLETT RD.
CARLTON ST.
PRIORY ST.
KINGS RD.
BATTLEDOWN APPROACH
STREET
LONDON
HALE'S ROAD
SANDFORD PARK
KENSHAM ROAD
SANDFORD MILL RD.
ROAD
A435 TO CIRENCESTER
CIRENCESTER RD.
A40 TO NORTHLEACH
LONDON ROAD
GREENWAY LANE
RYEWORTH ROAD
OLD BATH RD.
ROAD

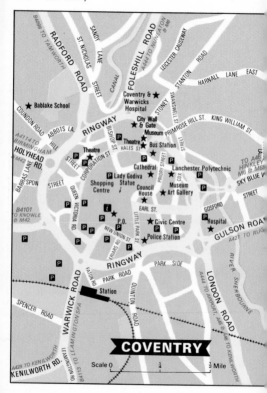

COVENTRY

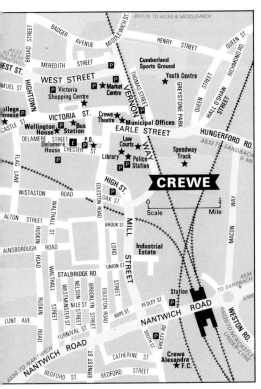

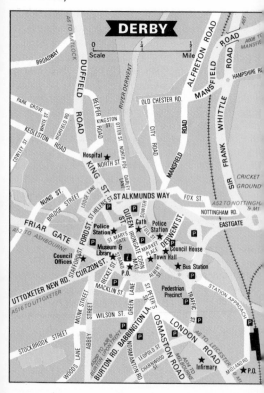

DERBY

Scale 0 ¼ ½ Mile

A610 TO MATLOCK
BROADWAY
DUFFIELD ROAD
BELPER ROAD
ALFRETON ROAD
MANSFIELD ROAD
A608 TO MANSF
WHITTLE ROAD
HAMPSHIRE RD
RIVER DERWENT
OLD CHESTER RD.
PARK GROVE
KEDLESTON ROAD
WHITE ST.
HIGHFIELD RD.
FOWLER ST.
KINGSTON ROAD
OTTER ST.
NORTH PDE.
DARLEY LANE
CITY ROAD
SIR FRANK
MANSFIELD
ROAD
CRICKET GROUND
Hospital ★
NORTH ST.
KING ST.
ST ALKMUNDS WAY
FOX ST.
A52 TO NOTTING'M & M1
NOTTINGHAM RD.
EASTGATE
NUNS ST.
BRIDGE STREET
LODGE LANE
ST HELENS ST.
FORD ST.
SOWTER
QUEEN ST.
Cath ★
FRIAR GATE
A52 TO ASHBOURNE
Police Station ■
ST MARYS GATE
IRONGATE
FULL ST.
DERWENT ST.
Police Station ■
Council House ★
Museum & Library ■
STAFFORD ST.
BECKET ST.
STRAND
CORN MKT.
MARKET PLACE
Town Hall ★
P
Council Offices ★
CURZON ST.
i
P.O. ■
ALBERT ST.
Bus Station ★
UTTOXETER NEW RD.
A516 TO UTTOXETER
MACKLIN ST.
GREEN LANE
ST PETER'S ST.
Pedestrian Precinct
TRAFFIC ST.
P
STATION APPROACH
MONK STREET
WILSON ST.
LONDON ROAD
A6 TO LEICESTER
STOCKBROOK STREET
WOODS LANE
ABBEY
BURTON RD.
BABBINGTON LA.
OSMASTON ROAD
LEOPOLD ST.
CHARNWOOD ST.
Infirmary ★
A514 TO MELBOURNE
MIDLAND RD.
P.O. ■
P

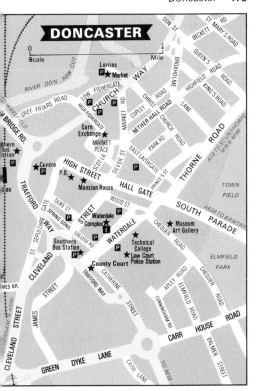

DONCASTER

0   ½   1
Scale   Mile

DON ST
ST MARY'S RD
BECKETT RD
QUEEN'S ROAD
HIGHFIELD ROAD
KING'S ROAD

RIVER DON NEW CUT

GREY FRIARS ROAD

W WAKEFIELD

BRIDGE RD

TO WAKEFIELD RD

TRAFFORD WAY

CLEVELAND STREET

RHAM & A1(M)

MES BR.

Lorries
Market
MARKET WAY

BROXHOLME

CHURCH
LOW FISHERGATE
HIGH FISHERGATE
CHRIST ROAD
COPLEY
NETHER HALL ROAD
LANE

Corn
Exchange
MARKET PLACE
MARKET RD
SILVER ST
EAST LAITHGATE
PARK RD
CHURCH ROAD
THORNE ROAD
A18 TO SCUNTHORPE
M18 & M180

Centre
P.O.
HIGH STREET
SCOT LA
PRINCE'S ST
HALL GATE
PRINCE'S ST

TOWN FIELD

Mansion House
WOOD ST
SOUTH PARADE
A638 TO BAWTRY

DUKE ST
STREET
GATE
SPRING GDNS
SEPULCHRE
ST
COLLEGE RD
Waterdale
Complex
WATERDALE
CHEQUER
Museum
Art Gallery
CHEQUER ROAD
ELMFIELD PARK

Southern
Bus Station
CLEVELAND
STREET
Technical
College
Law Court
Police Station
County Court

TRAFFORD WAY
CATHERINE
JAMES
STREET
STREET
APLEY ROAD
CUNNINGHAM RD
ELMFIELD ROAD
CHEQUER ROAD

GREEN DYKE LANE
CARR LANE
TO M18
CARR HOUSE ROAD
PALMER STREET

thern
Bus
Station

tion

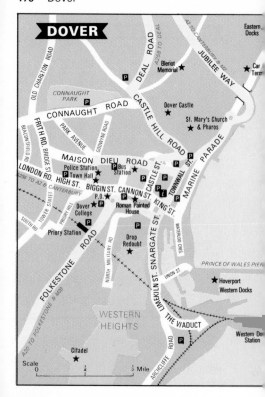

DOVER

Eastern Docks

A2 TO DEAL

JUBILEE WAY

Car Term

A258 TO DEAL

OLD CHARLTON ROAD

DEAL ROAD

Bleriot Memorial ★

A2 TO CANTERBURY B&D

CONNAUGHT PARK

P

CONNAUGHT ROAD

CASTLE HILL ROAD

Dover Castle ★

St. Mary's Church & Pharos ★

FRITH RD.

BEACONSFIELD RD.

PARK AVENUE

GODWYNE ROAD

BRIDGE ST.

MAISON DIEU ROAD

P

MARINE PARADE

LONDON RD.

A256 TO A2 & CANTERBURY

HIGH ST.

Police Station

P Town Hall

P Bus Station

BIGGIN ST. CANNON ST.

CASTLE ST.

TOWNWALL ST.

P.O. ★

P

Dover College ★

Roman Painted House

KING ST.

SOUTH RD.

TOWER STREET

PRIORY HILL

P

Priory Station

Drop Redoubt ★

WATERLOO CRES.

PRINCE OF WALES PIER

FOLKESTONE ROAD

A20 TO FOLKESTONE B MD

NORTH MILITARY RD.

LIMEKILN ST. SNARGATE ST.

UNION ST.

★ Hoverport
Western Docks

WESTERN HEIGHTS

THE VIADUCT

ROAD

Western Do Station

P

Citadel ★

ARCHCLIFFE RD.

Scale
0   ¼   ½ Mile

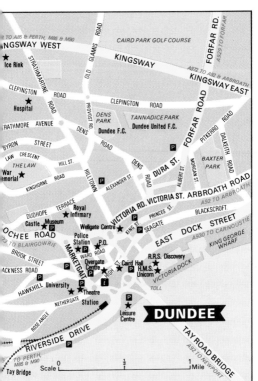

Dundee

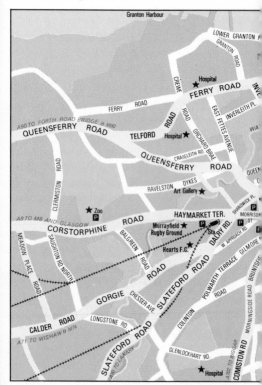

Granton Harbour

LOWER GRANTON

GRANTON ROAD

CREWE

Hospital ★

FERRY ROAD

INV

FERRY ROAD

EAST FETTES AVENUE

INVERLEITH PL.

A90 TO FORTH ROAD BRIDGE & M90

QUEENSFERRY ROAD

TELFORD ROAD

ROAD

WA

Hospital ★

ORCHARD BRAE

CRAIGLEITH RD.

QUEENSFERRY ROAD

QUEEN

C

RAVELSTON DYKES

Art Gallery ★

★ Zoo

CLERMISTON ROAD

P

HAYMARKET TER.

SHANDWICK PL.

P

MORRISON ST.

P

A8 TO M9 AND GLASGOW

CORSTORPHINE ROAD

Murrayfield ★
Rugby Ground

P

DALRY RD.

P

BALGREEN ROAD

Hearts F.C. ★

SLATEFORD ROAD

W. APPROACH RD.

GILMORE

SAUGHTON RD NORTH

MEADOW PLACE ROAD

ROAD

GORGIE

CHESSER AVE.

SLATEFORD ROAD

POLWARTH TERRACE

ROAD

MORNINGSIDE ROAD

BRUNTSFIE

GILMORE

CALDER ROAD

LONGSTONE RD.

COLINTON

A71 TO WISHAW & M74

SLATEFORD ROAD

A70 TO LANARK

GLENLOCKHART RD.

A702 TO BIGGAR

COMISTON RD.

Hospital ★

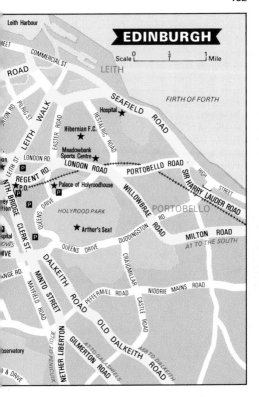

Leith Harbour

EDINBURGH

Scale 0 | ½ | 1 Mile

LEITH

FIRTH OF FORTH

COMMERCIAL ST

ROAD

STREET

LEITH WALK

PILRIG ST

EASTER ROAD

SEAFIELD ROAD

Hospital ★

Hibernian F.C. ★

RESTALRIG ROAD

Meadowbank Sports Centre ★

LONDON ROAD

LONDON RD.

REGENT RD.

PORTOBELLO ROAD

P.O. ★

★ Palace of Holyroodhouse

WILLOWBRAE RD

PORTOBELLO

SIR HARRY LAUDER ROAD

HIGH STREET

NORTH BRIDGE

HOLYROOD PARK

★ Arthur's Seat

QUEENS DRIVE

DUDDINGSTON ROAD

MILTON ROAD

A1 TO THE SOUTH

CLERK ST.

ospital

OWS

VE

QUEENS DRIVE

CRAIGMILLAR

GRANGE RD.

DALKEITH ROAD

MINTO STREET

MAYFIELD RD

PEFFERMILL ROAD

NIDDRIE MAINS ROAD

CASTLE ROAD

TO PENICUIK

NETHER LIBERTON

GILMERTON ROAD

OLD DALKEITH ROAD

A68 TO DALKEITH

A702 GALASHIELS

observatory

& DRIVE

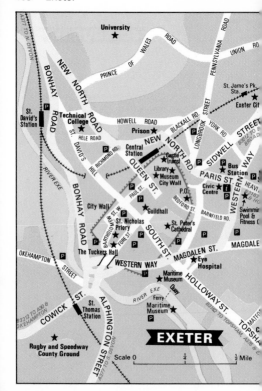

University ★

PRINCE OF WALES ROAD

PENNSYLVANIA ROAD

UNION RD.

A377 TO DEVON

NEW NORTH ROAD

BONHAY ROAD

St. Jame's Pk. Sta ★

Exeter Cit ★

St. David's Station

P

Technical College ★

HOWELL ROAD

BLACKALL RD.

LONGBROOK STREET

YORK RD.

B3212 TO BROAD

ST. DAVID'S HILL

HELE ROAD

RICHMOND RD.

Prison ★

NEW NORTH RD.

SIDWELL STREET

QUEEN ST.

P

Central Station ★

Castle (ruins) ★

Library ★

Museum ★

City Wall

PARIS ST.

Bus Station ★

P

P

HEAVI

B3123 TO

PAUL ST.

P.O. ★

Civic Centre ★

WESTERN WAY

City Wall ★

BARTHOLOMEW ST.

FORE ST.

Guildhall ★

St. Nicholas Priory ★

BEDFORD ST.

St. Peter's Cathedral ★

BARNFIELD RD.

Swimming Pool & Fitness C

BONHAY ROAD

OKEHAMPTON

The Tuckers Hall ★

SOUTH ST.

MAGDALEN ST.

MAGDALE

STREET

WESTERN WAY

Eye Hospital ★

RIVER EXE

P

Maritime Museum ★

HOLLOWAY ST.

B3182 TO TOPSHAM

B3212 TO A30 B OKEHAMPTON

COWICK ST.

ST. THOMAS ST.

St. Thomas Station ★

ALPHINGTON STREET

River Exe

Quay

Ferry

Maritime Museum ★

TOPSHA

A377 TO DEVON

Rugby and Speedway County Ground ★

EXETER

Scale 0   ¼   ½ Mile

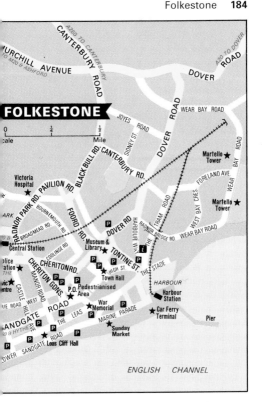

FOLKESTONE

A260 TO CANTERBURY
TO M20 & ASHFORD
URCHILL AVENUE
CANTERBURY ROAD
A20 TO DOVER
DOVER ROAD
DOVER
WEAR BAY ROAD
JOYES ROAD
ST. JOHN'S ST.
DOVER ROAD
0   ¼   Mile
cale
BLACK BULL RD. CANTERBURY RD.
WEAR BAY ROAD
Martello ★
Tower
FORELAND AVE
WEST BAY CRES.
WEAR BAY ROAD
Martello ★
Tower
Victoria ★
Hospital
PAVILION RD.
RAONOR PARK RD.
BOURNEMOUTH RD.
FOORD RD.
BROADMEAD RD.
DOVER RD
HARBOUR WAY
RADNOR BRIDGE RD.
TRAM ROAD
P
Museum & ★
Library
TONTINE ST.
t
ARK
P
B
Central Station
COOLINGE RD
P
HIGH ST.
THE STADE
Police
ation ★
THE
CHERITON RD.
CHERITON GDNS.
MANOR ROAD
P
★
Town Hall
HARBOUR
P
vic ★
ntre
CASTLE HILL AVE
P.O. Pedestrianised
Area
P
P
Harbour
Station
RIE ROAD WEST
P
★
War
Memorial
P
MARINE PARADE
★ Car Ferry
Terminal
Pier
ANDGATE
ROAD
THE LEAS
P
P
A59 B HYTHE AVE
P
P
Sunday
Market
OWER SANDGATE Leas Cliff Hall
P
P
ENGLISH   CHANNEL

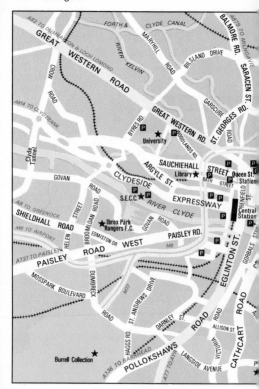

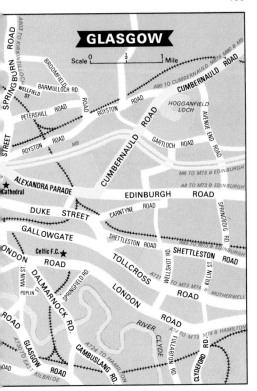

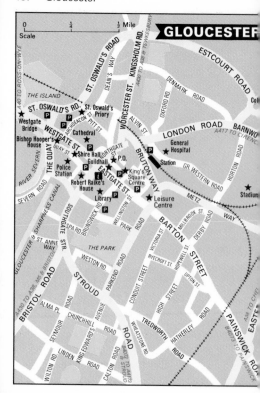

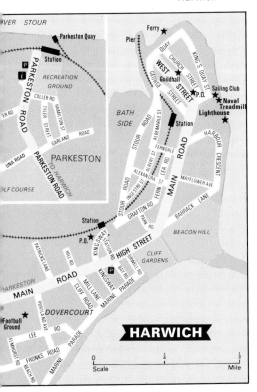

HARWICH

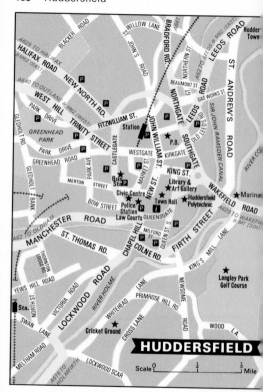

HUDDERSFIELD

Scale 0 ¼ ½ Mile

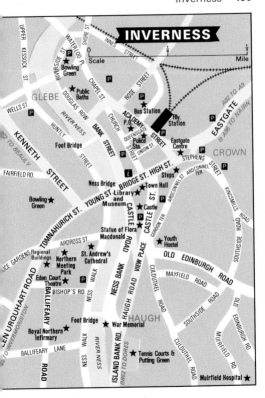

INVERNESS

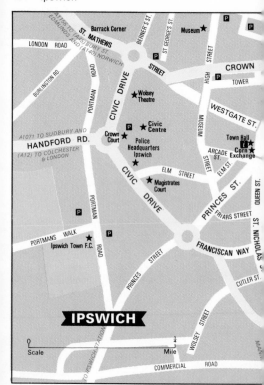

LONDON ROAD

A1156 TO BURY ST. EDMUNDS (A45) AND NORWICH (A140)

St. MATHEWS

Barrack Corner

BERNER'S ST.

ST. GEORGE'S ST.

Museum ★

P

P

BURLINGTON RD.

PORTMAN ROAD

CIVIC DRIVE

STREET

P

HIGH STREET

CROWN

TOWER

Wolsey Theatre ★

WESTGATE ST.

A1071 TO SUDBURY AND
HANDFORD RD.
(A12) TO COLCHESTER & LONDON

P

Crown Court

★ Civic Centre

Police Headquarters Ipswich

MUSEUM STREET

Town Hall ★
i Corn Exchange

ARCADE ST.

ELM STREET

ELM ST.

★

CIVIC DRIVE

★ Magistrates Court

PRINCES ST.

FRIARS STREET

QUEEN ST.

P

PORTMAN ROAD

PORTMANS WALK
★ Ipswich Town F.C.

P

FRANCISCAN WAY

ST. NICHOLAS S

PRINCES STREET

CUTLER ST.

MA

IPSWICH

0   ¼
Scale   Mile

WOLSEY STREET

TO IPSWICH STATION

COMMERCIAL ROAD

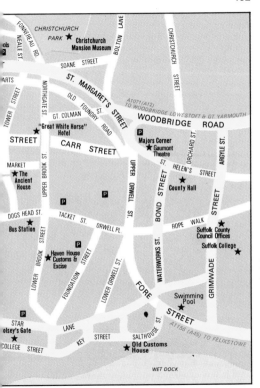

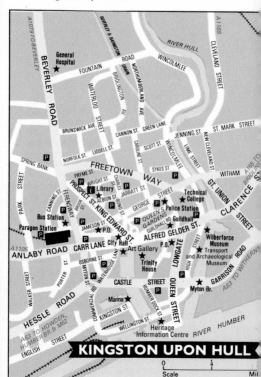

KINGSTON UPON HULL

Scale 0 — ¼ — ½ — Mil

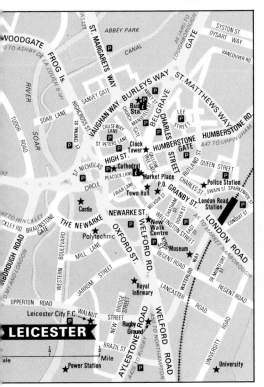

WOODGATE
TO ASHBY DE LA ZOUCH 8 M¹
ST. MARGARETS WAY
ABBEY PARK
CANAL
SYSTON ST.
DYSART WAY
VANCOUVER RD.
A6 (A46) TO LOUGHBOROUGH
A50/A6
FROG Is.

RIVER
SOAR
TUDOR ROAD
SOAR LANE
HIGHCROSS ST.
SANVEY GATE
VAUGHAN WAY
CAUSEWAY LANE
CHURCH GATE
ST. PETERS LANE
HIGH ST.
Clock Tower
ST. NICHOLAS CIRCLE
ST MATTHEWS WAY
BURLEYS WAY
Bus Sta.
BELGRAVE
CHARLES
LEE STREET
HUMBERSTONE RD.
A47 TO UPPINGHAM
HUMBERSTONE GATE
GALLOWTREE GATE
Cathedral
PEACOCK LANE
Market Place
FRIAR LANE
Town Hall
Castle
THE NEWARKE
BRAUNSTONE GATE
TO HINCKLEY
CKLEY RD.
BOULEVARD
MILL LANE
WESTERN
Polytechnic
NEWARKE ST.
OXFORD ST.
WELFORD
New Walk Centre
WELLINGTON STREET
DOVER ST.
EAST ST.
KING ST.
Museum
REGENT ROAD
P.O.
CHARLES ST.
GRANBY St.
Police Station
SWAIN ST.
SPARKENHOE ST.
London Road Station
CONDUIT ST.
A6 TO MARKET HARBOROUGH
LONDON ROAD
QUEEN STREET
RUTLAND ST.
BELVOIR ST.
CHATHAM ST.
DE MONTFORT
WAY
WATERLOO
LANCASTER
REGENT ROAD
ROAD
MBOROUGH ROAD
TO M1 AND LONDON
UPPERTON ROAD
Leicester City F.C.
WALNUT
JARROM STREET
NEW BRIDGE STREET
Royal Infirmary
AYLESTONE ROAD
Rugby Ground
A426 TO RUGBY
WELFORD ROAD
A46 TO NORTHAMPTON
UNIVERSITY ROAD
University
LEICESTER
¼   ½
ale   Mile
BRAZIL ST.
Power Station

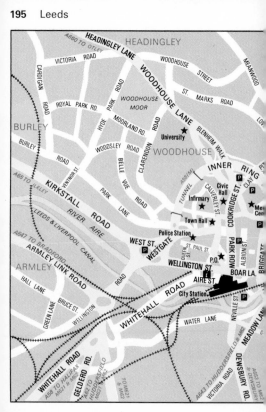

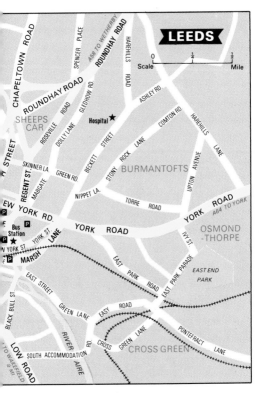

LEEDS

Scale 0 — ¼ — ½ Mile

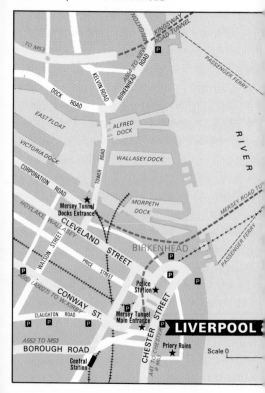

TO M53

KINGSWAY
ROAD TUNNEL

A554 TO NEW BRIGHTON

BIRKENHEAD ROAD

PASSENGER FERRY

KELVIN ROAD

DOCK ROAD

EAST FLOAT

ALFRED DOCK

TOWER ROAD

WALLASEY DOCK

RIVER

VICTORIA DOCK

CORPORATION ROAD

MORPETH DOCK

MERSEY ROAD TU

HOYLAKE WALLASEY

WATSON STREET

Mersey Tunnel
Docks Entrance ★

CLEVELAND STREET

PRICE STREET

BIRKENHEAD

PASSENGER FERRY

CONWAY ST.

A553 (A5027) TO W.KIRBY

Police
Station ★

P

CLAUGHTON ROAD

Mersey Tunnel
Main Entrance ★

CHESTER STREET

LIVERPOOL

A552 TO M53

BOROUGH ROAD

Priory Ruins ★

A41 TO CHESTER & M5

Scale 0

Central
Station

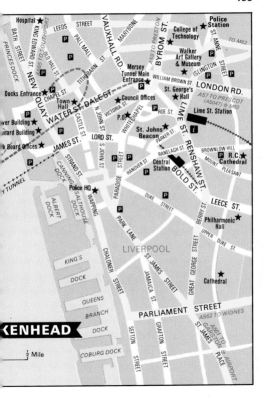

Hospital ★

LEEDS STREET

KING EDWARD ST.

PALL MALL

BATH STREET

PRINCES DOCK

NEW QUAY

Docks Entrance ★

Town Hall ★

CHAPEL ST.

WATER ST. DALE ST.

ver Building ★

unard Building ★

k Board Offices ★

JAMES ST.

CASTLE ST.

N. JOHN ST.

LORD ST.

S. JOHN ST.

VAUXHALL RD.

MARYBONE

LEEDS STREET

TITHEBARN ST.

VICTORIA ST.

BYROM ST.

College of Technology

PRESTON ST.

Mersey Tunnel Main Entrance ★

WILLIAM BROWN ST.

Council Offices ★

P.O. ★

WHITECHAPEL

★ Police Station

TO A62

ST. ANNE

Walker Art Gallery & Museum

ISLINGTON ST.

LONDON RD.

St. George's ★ Hall

ROE ST.

A57 TO PRESCOT (A5047) & M62

★ Lime St. Station

LIME ST.

St. Johns ★ Beacon

PARKER ST.

RENSHAW ST.

BROWNLOW HILL

R.C. ★ Cathedral

MOUNT PLEASANT

RANELAGH ST.

HANOVER ST.

Central Station

BOLD ST.

Y TUNNEL

Police HQ ★

SALTHOUSE DOCK

STRAND ST.

CANNING DOCK

WAPING

PARADISE STREET

HANOVER ST.

DUKE STREET

LEECE ST.

BERRY ST.

Philharmonic ★ Hall

UPPER DUKE ST.

ALBERT DOCK

PARK LANE

CHALONER STREET

LIVERPOOL

ST. JAMES STREET

GREAT GEORGE STREET

Cathedral ★

KING'S DOCK

QUEENS BRANCH DOCK

KENHEAD

½ Mile

COBURG DOCK

JAMAICA ST.

PARLIAMENT STREET

GRAFTON STREET

SEFTON STREET

A562 TO WIDNES

A561 TO GARSTON & AIRPORT

ST. JAMES PLACE

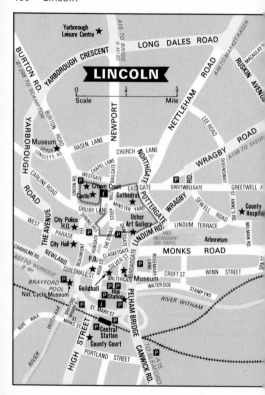

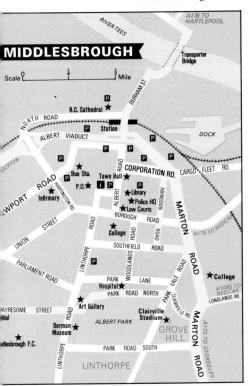

MIDDLESBROUGH

RIVER TEES

A178 TO HARTLEPOOL

Transporter Bridge

Scale 0 — ¼ — ½ Mile

NORTH ROAD

R.C. Cathedral ★

DURHAM ST.

P Station

ALBERT VIADUCT

DOCK

STOCKTON

NEWPORT ROAD

HARTINGTON RD.

P Bus Sta.

Town Hall ★

P.O. ★

Infirmary ★

ALBERT ROAD

CORPORATION RD.

CARGO FLEET RD.

★ Library

Police HQ ★

★ Law Courts

ABINGDON ROAD

MARTON ROAD

BOROUGH ROAD

UNION STREET

College ★

LINTHORPE ROAD

WOODLANDS ROAD

ROAD

ROAD

SOUTHFIELD ROAD

A175 TO REDCAR

PARLIAMENT ROAD

PARK LANE

Hospital ★

PARK ROAD NORTH

PARK VALE ROAD

CLAIRVILLE ROAD

★ College

A1085 TO REDCAR LONGLANDS RD.

AYRESOME STREET

★ Art Gallery

Clairville Stadium ★

ALBERT PARK

GROVE HILL

MARTON ROAD

A172 TO STOKESLEY

★ Dorman Museum

★ ddlesbrough F.C.

LINTHORPE ROAD

PARK ROAD SOUTH

LINTHORPE

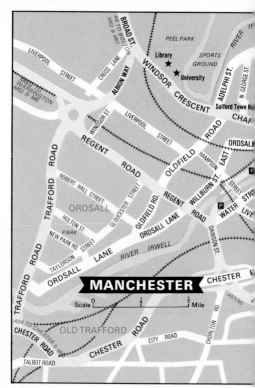

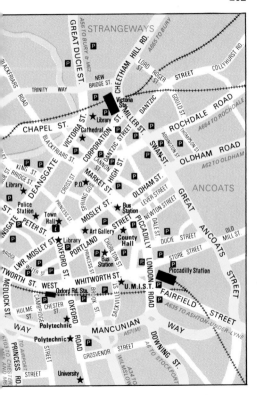

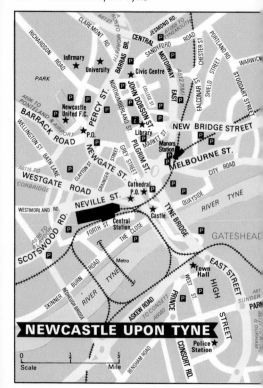

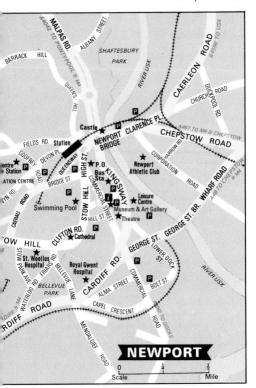

NEWPORT

Scale

0   ¼   ½ Mile

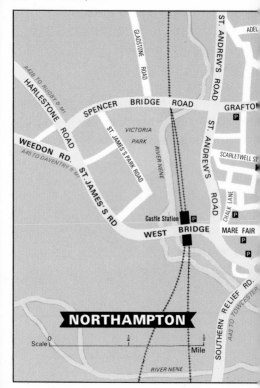

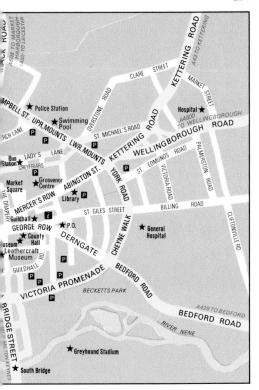

BACK ROAD

A508 TO MARKET
HARBOROUGH
A801 TO LEICESTER

KETTERING ROAD

A4310 KETTERING

CLARE STREET

KETTERING ROAD

MARKET STREET

★ Police Station

CAMPBELL ST. UPR. MOUNTS

OFFERSTONE ROAD

ST. MICHAEL'S ROAD

Hospital ★

A4500
TO WELLINGBOROUGH

★ Swimming
Pool

LWR. MOUNTS

KETTERING ROAD

WELLINGBOROUGH ROAD

CHURCH LANE

LADY'S LANE

Bus
Station

GREYFRIARS

ABINGTON ST.

YORK ROAD

ST. EDMUNDS ROAD

PALMERSTON ROAD

Market
Square

★ Grosvenor
Centre

VICTORIA ROAD

MERCER'S ROW

★ Library

BILLING ROAD

ST. GILES STREET

CLIFTONVILLE RD

THE DRAPERY

Guildhall ★

ℹ

CHEYNE WALK

George Row

★ P.O.

★ General
Hospital

★ County
Hall

DERNGATE

Museum

Leathercraft
Museum ★

GUILDHALL RD

BEDFORD ROAD

VICTORIA PROMENADE

BECKETTS PARK

A428 TO BEDFORD

BEDFORD ROAD

BRIDGE STREET

A508 TO MILTON KEYNES

RIVER NENE

★ Greyhound Stadium

★ South Bridge

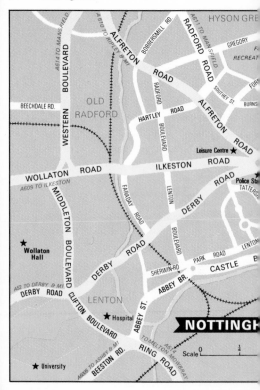

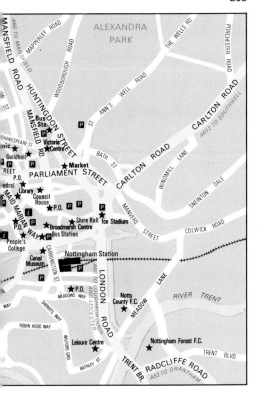

NORWICH

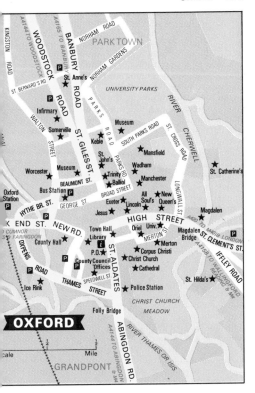

KINGSTON ROAD

A4165 TO BANBURY

NORHAM ROAD

PARKTOWN

A4144 TO WOODSTOCK

WOODSTOCK ROAD

BANBURY ROAD

NORHAM GARDENS

ST. BERNARD'S RD

★ St. Anne's

UNIVERSITY PARKS

WALTON STREET

P
Infirmary ★

P
★ Somerville

ST. GILES ST.

PARKS ROAD

RIVER CHERWELL

★ Museum

★ Keble

SOUTH PARKS ROAD

ST. CROSS ROAD

★ St. John's

★ Mansfield

Worcester ★

★ Museum

BEAUMONT ST.

Oxford Station P

Bus Station P

GEORGE ST.

★ Trinity
★ Balliol

BROAD STREET

★ Wadham

★ Manchester

★ St. Catherine's

PARKS ROAD

HYTHE BR. ST.

Exeter ★
★ Jesus

★ All Soul's
Lincoln ★

★ New
★ Queen's

LONGWALL ST.

A420 TO A40/B TO LONDON

Magdalen ★

K END ST. NEW RD.

Town Hall
Library i

Oriel ★ Univ. ★

HIGH STREET

Magdalen Bridge

ST. CLEMENT'S ST.

County Hall

OXPENS

P

County Council
Offices

P.O. ★

MERTON'S

★ Merton

★ Corpus Christi

A4158 TO WALLINGFORD 8 M4

IFFLEY ROAD

ROAD

★ Ice Rink

THAMES

ST. ALDATES

SPEEDWELL ST.

STREET

Christ Church ★
★ Cathedral

★ Police Station

★ St. Hilda's

TO CUMNOR
TO FARINGDON

★ Folly Bridge

CHRIST CHURCH MEADOW

OXFORD

cale

Mile

GRANDPONT

RIVER THAMES OR ISIS

A4144 TO ABINGDON

ABINGDON RD.

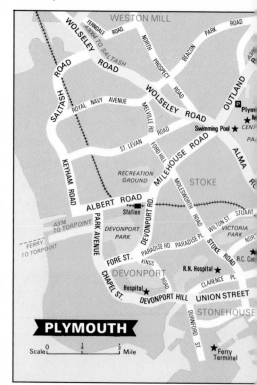

PLYMOUTH

Scale 0 — 1/4 — 1/2 Mile

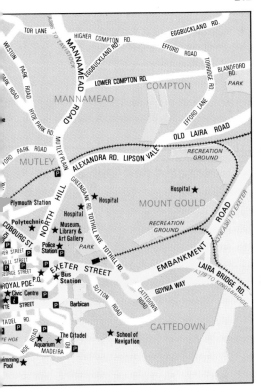

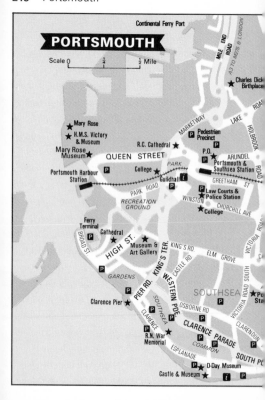

PORTSMOUTH

Continental Ferry Port

Scale 0   ¼   ½ Mile

★ Charles Dickens Birthplace

★ Mary Rose
★ H.M.S. Victory & Museum
Mary Rose Museum ★
Portsmouth Harbour Station

QUEEN STREET
★ R.C. Cathedral
College ★
Guildhall ★
PARK ROAD
RECREATION GROUND

Pedestrian Precinct
P.O. ★
Portsmouth & Southsea Station
ARUNDEL ST
GREETHAM ST
★ Law Courts & Police Station
WINSTON
CHURCHILL AVE
★ College

MARKETWAY
LAKE ROAD
HOLBROOK
MILE END ROAD
A3 TO M275 & LONDON

Ferry Terminal
Cathedral ★
HIGH ST.
Museum & Art Gallery ★
KING'S TER.
BROAD ST
PIER RD.
GARDENS
KING'S RD.
CASTLE RD
ELM GROVE
WESTERN PDE.
OSBORNE RD

Clarence Pier ★

R.N. War Memorial ★
CLARENCE
SOUTHSEA
ESPLANADE
CLARENCE PARADE
COMMON
SOUTHSEA
VICTORIA ROAD SOUTH
CLARENDON
SOUTH PE

★ D-Day Museum
Castle & Museum ★

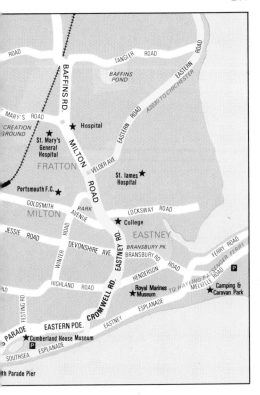

ROAD

TANGIER ROAD

BAFFINS RD.

BAFFINS POND

EASTERN ROAD

EASTERN ROAD

A2030 TO CHICHESTER

MARY'S ROAD

★ Hospital

CREATION GROUND

★ St. Mary's General Hospital

MILTON ROAD

EASTERN ROAD

FRATTON

VELDER AVE.

St. James ★ Hospital

Portsmouth F.C. ★

GOLDSMITH

PARK AVENUE

LOCKSWAY ROAD

MILTON

ROAD

★ College

EASTNEY

JESSIE ROAD

DEVONSHIRE AVE.

BRANSBURY PK.

EASTNEY RD.

BRANSBURY RD.

ROAD

FERRY ROAD

WINTER

HENDERSON

TO HAYLING PASSENGER FERRY

MELVILLE ROAD

P

HIGHLAND ROAD

CROMWELL RD.

Royal Marines ★ Museum

★ Camping & Caravan Park

AD

FESTING RD.

EASTERN PDE.

EASTNEY

ESPLANADE

S PARADE

★ Cumberland House Museum

SOUTHSEA

P

ESPLANADE

th Parade Pier

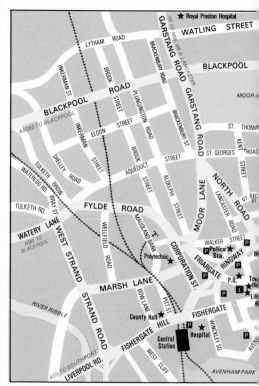

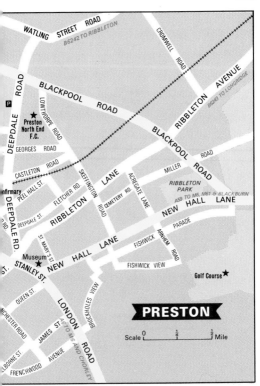

PRESTON

Scale 0 — ¼ — ½ Mile

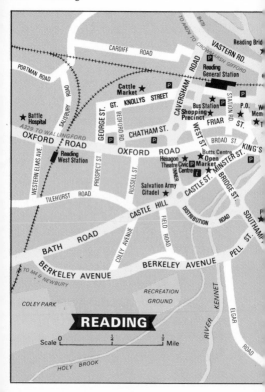

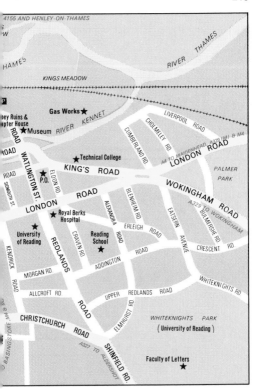

TO A4155 AND HENLEY-ON-THAMES

RIVER THAMES

HAMES

KINGS MEADOW

★ Gas Works

Abbey Ruins & Chapter House
★ Museum   RIVER KENNET

CHOLMLEY RD

LIVERPOOL ROAD

A4 TO MAIDENHEAD, A320 (M4) & M4

CUMBERLAND RD

LONDON ROAD

PALMER PARK

ROAD

WATLINGTON ST.

ROAD

★ Technical College
KING'S   ROAD

ELDON RD

★ P.O.

LONDON   ROAD

SIDMOUTH ST.

WOKINGHAM ROAD

A329 TO WOKINGHAM

BLENHEIM RD

ALEXANDRA   ROAD

EASTERN   AVENUE

BULMERSHE RD

CRESCENT   RD

★ Royal Berks
Hospital

ERLEIGH   ROAD

★
University
of Reading

KENDRICK   ROAD

REDLANDS

CRAVEN RD

★
Reading
School

ADDINGTON   ROAD

ROAD

MORGAN RD

ALLCROFT RD

ROAD

UPPER   REDLANDS   ROAD

WHITEKNIGHTS RD

CHRISTCHURCH   ROAD

A4 TO BASINGSTOKE, M4 & M3

ELMHURST RD

A327 TO ALDERSHOT

SHINFIELD RD.

WHITEKNIGHTS   PARK
(University of Reading)

★ Faculty of Letters

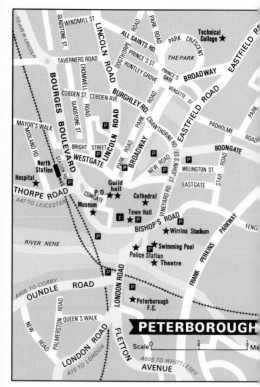

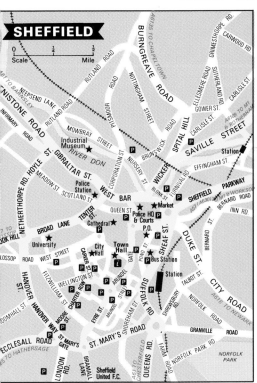

SHEFFIELD

0   Scale   ⅓   Mile

A616 TO BARNSLEY
'NISTONE ROAD
INFIRMARY   ROAD
NEEPSEND LANE
NETHERTHORPE RD. HOYLE ST.
MEADOW ST.
MOWBRAY   STREET
Industrial Museum
RIVER DON
ST. GIBRALTAR ST.
SCOTLAND ST.
JOK HILL
7 TO
BROAD LANE
TENTER ST.
University
WEST STREET
GLOSSOP   ROAD
HANOVER ST.
DOOMHALL ST.   HANOVER WAY
MOORE ST.
FITZWILLIAM ST.   CHARTER ST.
WELLINGTON   STREET
EYRE ST.
CARVER ST.
ARUNDEL
STREET
ST. MARY'S
GATE
ECCLESALL ROAD
A510 TO HATHERSAGE
LONDON   RD.
BRAMALL   LANE
ST. MARY'S   ROAD
SHOREHAM ST.
Sheffield United F.C.
QUEENS   ROAD
A61 TO CHESTERFIELD

BURNGREAVE   ROAD
A6135 TO CHAPELTOWN
RUTLAND   ROAD
RUTLAND ROAD
PITSMOOR   ROAD
NOTTINGHAM   STREET
BRUNSWICK
NURSERY ST.
CORPORATION ST.
WEST BAR
Police Station
QUEEN ST.
Cathedral
City Hall
Town Hall
CARVER ST.

GRIMESTHORPE RD.   CARWOOD RD.
ELLESMERE ROAD
SUTHERLAND RD.
GOWER ST.
CARLISLE ST.
SPITAL HILL
CARLISLE ST.
SAVILLE   STREET
Station
EFFINGHAM ST.
WICKER
BLONK ST.
FURNIVAL RD.
SHEFFIELD
A57 (A630) TO WORKSOP
BERNARD ROAD
PARKWAY
INN RD.
Market
Police HQ & Courts
P.O.
GATE
Bus Station
SHEAF ST.
DUKE ST.
BERNARD   ST.
Station
TALBOT ST.
CITY ROAD
A616 TO NEWARK
SHREWSBURY   ST.
NORFOLK   ST.
NORFOLK   ROAD
GRANVILLE   ROAD
SUFFOLK RD.
FARM   RD.
QUEENS   RD.
NORFOLK PARK RD.
NORFOLK PARK
A61 TO
CHESTERFIELD

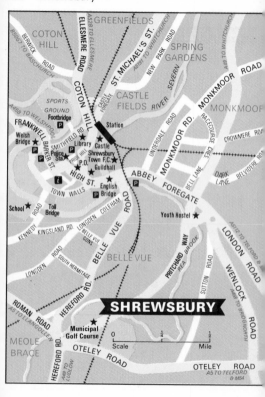

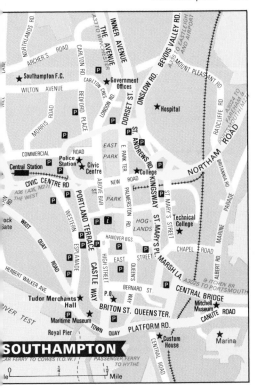

SOUTHAMPTON

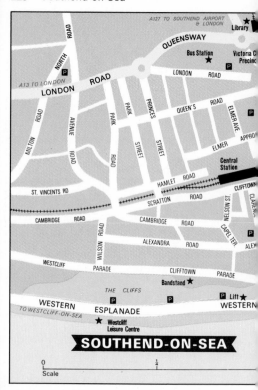

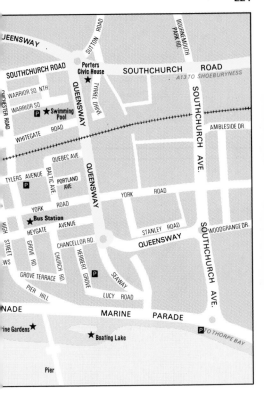

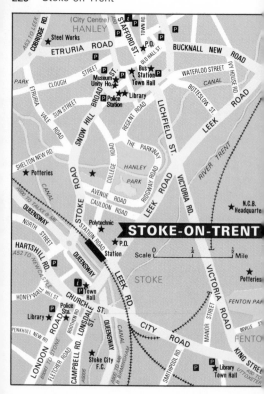

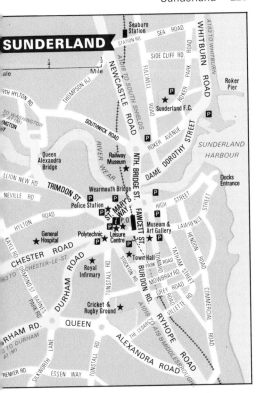

SUNDERLAND

Seaburn Station
SEA ROAD
STATION RD.
SIDE CLIFF RD.
WHITBURN ROAD
A183 TO WHITBURN

Roker Pier

Mile

NEWCASTLE ROAD
A1018 TO SOUTH SHIELDS
FULLWELL
ROKER PARK ROAD

NORTH HYLTON RD
THOMPSON RD.
TO WASHINGTON A1231
WASHINGTON WAY

SOUTHWICK ROAD
ROKER AVENUE
Sunderland F.C.

Queen Alexandra Bridge
RIVER WEAR
Railway Museum
DAME DOROTHY STREET
SUNDERLAND HARBOUR

STALLION NEW RD
TRIMDON ST.
NEVILLE RD.
NORTH BRIDGE ST.
Docks Entrance

Wearmouth Bridge
Police Station
HIGH STREET
STREET

HYLTON ROAD
ST. MARY'S WAY
P.O.
FAWCETT ST.
LAWRENCE STREET

General Hospital
Polytechnic
Leisure Centre
Museum & Art Gallery
HENDON ROAD

CHESTER ROAD
A183 TO CHESTER-LE-ST.
OSMONDSBY
ST. BARNES PARK RD.
DURHAM ROAD
TUNSTALL RD.
Town Hall
STOCKTON RD.
TOWARD ROAD
PARK ROAD
MOWBRAY RD.
TATHAM STREET
COMMERCIAL ROAD

Royal Infirmary
BURDON RD.
GREY ROAD
VILLETTE RD.

KAYLL RD.
Cricket & Rugby Ground
THE CEDARS
A1018 TO A19 B MIDDLESBROUGH

RHOPE ROAD

DURHAM RD.
A690 TO DURHAM
A1(M)
QUEEN
SILKSWORTH LANE
TUNSTALL RD.
ALEXANDRA ROAD

PREMIER RD.
ESSEN WAY
RYHOPE ROAD

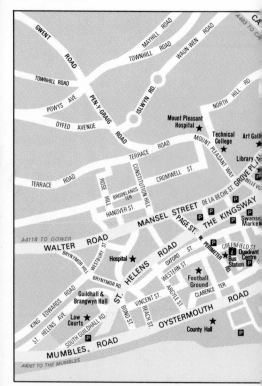

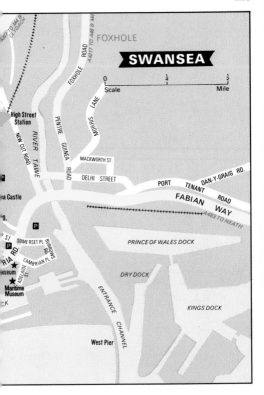

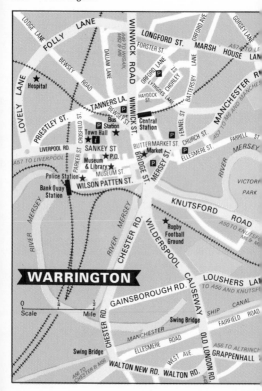

WARRINGTON

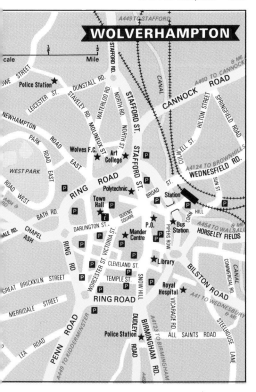

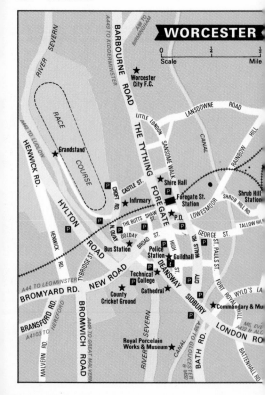

WORCESTER

Scale: 0 — ¼ — ½ Mile

A449 TO KIDDERMINSTER
A38 TO BIRMINGHAM

RIVER SEVERN

BARBOURNE ROAD

★ Worcester City F.C.

LANSDOWNE ROAD

LITTLE LONDON

SANSOME WALK

THE TYTHING

CANAL

RAINBOW HILL

RACE COURSE

★ Grandstand

A443 TO LUDLOW

HENWICK RD.

HYLTON ROAD

CASTLE ST.

CROFT RD.

★ Shire Hall

FOREGATE

Foregate St. Station ■

● Shrub Hill Station

SHRUB HILL RD.

★ Infirmary

THE BUTTS

SHAW ST.

N. QUAY

DOLDAY

P.O.

LOWESMOOR

TALLOW HILL

A44 TO LEOMINSTER

HENWICK RD.

TYBRIDGE ST.

Bus Station ■

BROAD ST.

Police Station ■

HIGH ST.

ST. SWITHIN

Guildhall ★

GEORGE ST.

ST. PAUL'S ST.

FORT ROYAL

WYLD'S LA.

NEW ROAD

BROMYARD RD.

Technical College ★

DEANSWAY

CITY

SIDBURY

★ Cathedral

★ County Cricket Ground

★ Commandery & Mus

LONDON RO

BRANSFORD RD.

BROMWICH ROAD

A4103 TO HEREFORD

A449 TO GREAT MALVERN

RIVER SEVERN

★ Royal Porcelain Works & Museum

CANAL

A449 TO GLOUCESTER & M50

BATH RD.

MS, EVE
MKE & ALC

BATTENHALL RD

MALVERN RD.

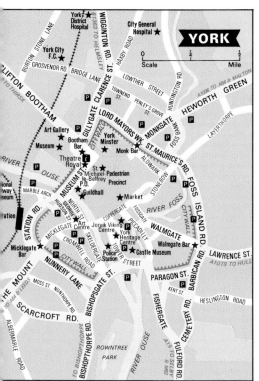